Cambridge Elements

Elements in Music Since 1945
edited by
Mervyn Cooke
University of Nottingham

CAGE, NONO AND 1960S HAUNTOLOGY

Sonic Ghosts

Clare Lesser
Independent Scholar

Shaftesbury Road, Cambridge CB2 8EA, United Kingdom

One Liberty Plaza, 20th Floor, New York, NY 10006, USA

477 Williamstown Road, Port Melbourne, VIC 3207, Australia

314–321, 3rd Floor, Plot 3, Splendor Forum, Jasola District Centre, New Delhi – 110025, India

103 Penang Road, #05–06/07, Visioncrest Commercial, Singapore 238467

Cambridge University Press is part of Cambridge University Press & Assessment, a department of the University of Cambridge.

We share the University's mission to contribute to society through the pursuit of education, learning and research at the highest international levels of excellence.

www.cambridge.org
Information on this title: www.cambridge.org/9781009487979

DOI: 10.1017/9781009488006

© Clare Lesser 2025

This publication is in copyright. Subject to statutory exception and to the provisions of relevant collective licensing agreements, no reproduction of any part may take place without the written permission of Cambridge University Press & Assessment.

When citing this work, please include a reference to the DOI 10.1017/9781009488006

First published 2025

A catalogue record for this publication is available from the British Library

ISBN 978-1-009-48797-9 Hardback
ISBN 978-1-009-48795-5 Paperback
ISSN 2632-7791 (online)
ISSN 2632-7783 (print)

Additional resources for this publication at www.Cambridge.org/Lesser

Cambridge University Press & Assessment has no responsibility for the persistence or accuracy of URLs for external or third-party internet websites referred to in this publication and does not guarantee that any content on such websites is, or will remain, accurate or appropriate.

For EU product safety concerns, contact us at Calle de José Abascal, 56, 1°, 28003 Madrid, Spain, or email eugpsr@cambridge.org

Cage, Nono and 1960s Hauntology

Sonic Ghosts

Elements in Music Since 1945

DOI: 10.1017/9781009488006
First published online: November 2025

Clare Lesser
Independent Scholar
Author for correspondence: Clare Lesser, clarelesser76@gmail.com

Abstract: 'What does it mean to follow a ghost?' Posing this question in *Specters of Marx* (1993), Jacques Derrida introduces the philosophical concept of 'hauntology' and the 'medium of the media' through the Shakespearian trope that time is 'out of joint'. Replete with ghostly crackles, hiss, pops and static, analogue media occupied a pivotal role in experimental music and praxis in the twentieth century, particularly during the 1960s, when composers such as John Cage and Luigi Nono systematically exploited the affordances of records and tape in composition and performance. Exploring hauntology's ghostly interplay with music and technology, this Element considers lost futures, past usage and future implications for hauntological music from the late 1930s to the twenty-first century.

Keywords: hauntology, Cage, Nono, records, tape

© Clare Lesser 2025

ISBNs: 9781009487979 (HB), 9781009487955 (PB), 9781009488006 (OC)
ISSNs: 2632-7791 (online), 2632-7783 (print)

Contents

1 Introduction — 1

2 Situating Hauntology — 2

3 Cage and the Phonograph — 25

4 Nono and Tape — 49

  Afterword — 74

  References — 76

1 Introduction

Spool! [*Pause.*] Spooool!
— Samuel Beckett, *Krapp's Last Tape*[1]

In the opening pages of *Specters of Marx*, Derrida (2006, p.10) asks his readers: 'What does it mean to follow a ghost?' On first reading, the question seems abstract, perhaps arbitrary. After all, what indeed does it mean to follow a ghost, and why would we be following a ghost in the first place? Two keywords – *ghost* and *follow* – will help begin unravelling this conundrum. Both immediately foreground temporality, a ghost is the return of something from the past, while to follow must imply that there is something *to* follow, something in front, in the future; and yet, if we are following, that future is also attached to our present, while the ghost is situated in the past. Thus, a fragmentary 'spectral moment', as Derrida would call it, occupies time that is 'out of joint', where past, present and future are no longer separate and sequential, but locked in a restless and unstable 'now'. But what else, apart from spooks and phantoms, does the ghost suggest? The concept of the ghost conjures up images of the lost and the missing, it transports us to the realms of memory, while also evoking the world of sepia-tinted photographs and the crackle of old records, the hiss of decaying tape, the smell of mould, damp and the decaying plastic that is so redolent of obsolete media. Such ghostly media, although once the technological hope of the future, now allow us to traverse a landscape of traces through decaying recordings of events long past, derived from texts that are still older. A shellac record allows us literally to hold the past in our hands, endlessly turning, repeating itself like Krapp's spooling tapes. Derrida continues his line of thought by asking, 'and what if this came down to being followed by it . . . persecuted perhaps by the very chase we are leading? . . . what seems to be out front, the future, comes back in advance: from the past, from the back' (Derrida, 2006, p.10). Herein lies the basis for contemporary understandings of hauntology, particularly in its interface with analogue technologies of recording and dissemination.

Derrida remarks, 'everything begins by the apparition of a specter. More precisely by the *waiting* for this apparition' (2006, p.2). In the spirit of Derrida's 'waiting', Section 2 of this Element introduces hauntology as a philosophical and 'spectral' concept – from Derrida to Mark Fisher et al. and beyond – and some of the ways in which it operates in musical praxis. Section 3 streamlines the hauntological content from Section 2, mapping content derived from a smaller number of authors onto selected mid-century (and later) works by John Cage

---

[1] Beckett, 1990, p.216.

where recorded discs – from the shellac phonograph to the vinyl LP – and their players are intrinsic parts of the total musical experience. Using *33⅓* as a key example of the genre, I reflect on Cage's use of the record as an agent of indeterminacy, and his apparent indifference to its content in some of the pieces from this period. Section 4 considers selected examples of music involving magnetic tape by Luigi Nono from the same period, focusing on *La fabbrica illuminata* as a key example, and examining the role of magnetic tape as a political and social tool for Nono. The Element concludes with a brief consideration of possible implications for analogue technology and historically informed performance in the twenty-first century, asking 'What now for these analogue letters to the future?' I would like to thank Kacper Madejek for invaluable research assistance in the early days of this project, and David Lesser for continual support throughout its development.

2 Situating Hauntology

> That is what we would be calling here a hauntology.
> – Jacques Derrida (*Specters of Marx*)[2]

Hauntology: a popular buzzword of the late twentieth and early twenty-first century, dragging fields as diverse as landscape studies, sound studies, spectral studies, retro studies, art, music, theatre, film studies, cultural studies and more into its ever-increasing orbit, while itself being subsumed into wider obsessions with the ghostly and the spectral, nostalgia, revenants and a past that simply will not let go. Dominated by sampling, library music, vintage records, British psychedelia, decaying tape and public broadcasting materials, the genre that has since become best known as hauntological pop music experienced something of a boom in the late 1990s and early noughties, when chillwave, retrofuturism, glo-fi, hypnagogic pop, Burial, Ghost Box, Belbury Poly, the Caretaker and William Basinski found themselves thrust into the limelight of popular consciousness. Is hauntology limited to popular music styles, and just how far back can its practical manifestations be traced? Originating during the 1990s in the work of the French Algerian philosopher Jacques Derrida (1930–2004), hauntology as a term has subsequently evolved into an influential and much more broadly construed creative strategy, moving across the arts and into wider twenty-first century culture, while being retrospectively applied to music from the mid twentieth century and earlier.

Because the field is complex and replete with circumlocutions, I feel a loose definition of hauntology in its current totality will prove useful. Derrida's initial

---

[2] Derrida, 2006, p.202.

concept problematises the nature of ontology, instead proposing a 'hauntology' that is neither 'being' nor 'non-being'. Using a quotation from Shakespeare's *Hamlet* as a point of reference, Derridean hauntology engages with time and place that are both 'out of joint' and all the repercussions implied by that statement. The figure of the ghost – or revenant – as representative of the 'no longer' or 'not yet' is emblematic of a past – particularly an archived past – that endlessly repeats, in conjunction with futures that are lost. Subsequent writers have developed Derrida's initial concept further, allowing the term to proliferate across the arts in twenty-first-century practice and discourse. Key points include:

- Revenants, ghosts, repetition, time that is out of joint, the medium of the media, techno-tele-iconicity, techno-tele-discursivity, communication without contact, spatial and temporal undecidability, decentring, liminality.
- Lost futures; the 'no longer' and 'not yet'.
- Analogue technology; crackle, whine, static and hiss; crate digging; decay.
- Nostalgia, memory, inheritance, digital archives, loss.

Although we may think of hauntology as applying exclusively to the late twentieth century – since Derrida's first use was in the 1990s – in fact, as well as encompassing contemporary practices, the term has also been applied retrospectively to earlier cultural and artistic fields. Considering the plethora of ghosts and spirits that greet the reader of Derrida's text, from the title, *Specters of Marx*, onwards, coupled with the almost totemic opening of Marx and Engel's 1848 *Manifesto of the Communist Party*, 'A spectre is haunting Europe – the spectre of Communism' (1985, p.78), it is hardly surprising that one of these fields should be the ghost story, a genre that, although going back centuries, found particular favour in the nineteenth century, as technologies of speed, remote communication and recording – railways, telephone, wireless telegraphy, mechanical recording and such – were ushering in seismic changes to traditional concepts of time and place and the ways in which society thought about itself and those who had gone before. The growth in scientific fields such as archaeology and palaeontology, coupled with Charles Darwin's groundbreaking theories of evolution,[3] further widened the already growing rupture in concepts of linear narrative time. A positive mania for 'isms' swept across nineteenth-century Europe and the United States – occultism, mesmerism and spiritualism – all of which were representative of both a yearning for a deep, often rose-tinted, past and a desire to communicate with it via modern technology's 'ghosts in the machine'. High infant mortality, cholera epidemics, non-existent industrial worker safety protocols and poverty led to 'a powerful and

---

[3] Darwin published *On the Origin of Species by Means of Natural Selection, or the Preservation of Favoured Races in the Struggle for Life* in 1859.

newly emergent sense of the supernatural' (Coverley, 2020, p.25) manifested in literature, theatre, art and the ultimate performance event, the séance. Celebrities, including Charles Dickens, contributed to the rising popularity of the ghost story in no small way – despite his well-publicised scepticism. His *A Christmas Carol* (1843), with its three ghosts – Christmas past, present and future – is an illuminating narration of contemporary hauntological tropes. Attempts to expose fraudulent practitioners, even if successful, often came to nothing, instead having the opposite effect, driving public desire for the supernatural to even greater heights. Of course, ghosts are perfect vessels through which to project the subconscious desire to reset 'lost futures' by rectifying past wrongs and giving justice to historical victims, even when they are already dead.

Building on an already extant tradition of ghostly unreliable narrators, found objects – letters, diaries, lost archives[4] and records, in the nineteenth century, radio and recordings in the twentieth – and the eighteenth-century epistolary novel, the ghost story is fertile ground for the hauntologist. So how can ghosts help us understand hauntology? They embody memory and loss, they problematise a linear narrative sense of time and they also unsettle our sense of place, and are powerful foci for nostalgia. According to Coverley (2020, p.49), they problematise 'the clash between two different and incompatible forms of temporality . . . the cyclical time of mythology . . . and . . . the linear historical time of a Christian society on the cusp of secular modernity'. Coverley addresses this hauntological confrontation with deep, cyclical pagan time and its power to rupture the present in the ghost stories of Vernon Lee and Arthur Machin; but of course, this trope occurs in many other ghost stories from the period. E. F. Benson's 'Negotium Perambulans' relates the negative influence of the past – via buried memories that reside in symbolic objects – and its hideous reoccurrence in the present. M. R. James's obsessive historians, archaeologists and other miscellaneous – typically, although not exclusively – Edwardian scholars frequently fall into these ruptures, and his classic tales 'The Ash-Tree' and 'A Warning to the Curious' confront the malevolent legacy of ancient injustices centred on witchcraft and pre-Christian relics, while John Buchan's 'The Wind in the Portico: Mr Henry Nightingale's Story' covers similar ground. H. P. Lovecraft's weird tales tend to coalesce around fractured times in colonial New England, non-US-based scientific and archaeological investigations – such as 'The Nameless City' – that unearth terrible truths and, in 'The Outsider',

---

[4] The Black Meadow Archive collective has created a hauntological alternative history of the North York Moors, replete with 'weird' happenings, comprising photographs, letters, police reports, myths, legends and other peculiar found objects. The accompanying sound art and music is a powerful component of the archive. See the *Black Meadow Archive Volume 1* at https://thesoullessparty-cis.bandcamp.com/album/the-black-meadow-archive-volume-1.

a humanoid being from a parallel reality that becomes a 'living' ghost after breaking through a physical barrier between the two worlds. As with so many of these tales, 'found' or missing documents are often pivotal carriers of plot: Lovecraft's 'The Case of Charles Dexter Ward' and M. R. James's 'The Treasure of Abbot Thomas' and 'The Tractate Midoth' use this device, while W. Hope-Hodgson's classic tale *The House on the Borderland* – where space and time rupture to devastating effect – unfolds via the pages of a retrieved diary. The Black Meadow Archive collective centres around the mysterious archives of one Roger Mullins, erstwhile researcher and professor at the University of York, who has since disappeared in highly mysterious circumstances. The stories move from deep, cyclical pagan time ('Legend of the White Horse' and 'The Blackberry Ghost') to the thin veneer of supposed rationality of the nineteenth and twentieth centuries ('A Dead Man on the Moor' and 'The Village Under the Lake') and colliding temporal ruptures and maze-like quests in the essentially timeless folk horror tradition ('The Blackberry Swim'). Death in conjunction with some variety of remote communication technology that invariably allows the voices of the dead to be heard is another frequent trope. The reclusive physicist Sir James Horton's experiments with an adapted gramophone contraption, inserted into the skull of recent victims of violence, that allows the dead to speak in E. F. Benson's 'And the Dead Spake . . .' is one such example of the technologically aided revenant, while ghostly voices transmitted over radio frequencies in A. G. Birch's novella *The Moon Terror* (1922) are eventually revealed to be extraterrestrial in origin. Perhaps the most tragic manifestation of the ghostly power of memory occurs not in literature but in music, in the work of James Leyland Kirby's alter ego The Caretaker, whose vast hauntological exploration of Alzheimer's disease through heavily sampled 1930s ballroom records is a case study in the disintegration of the self into the eternal now that is the ghost world of erased memory. Added to these technologically aided temporal disjunctions are examples where inanimate objects – stones, houses and altars – act as conduits or recording devices, invariably of evil acts, such as in Jeremy Burnham and Trevor Ray's *Children of the Stones* (1977) and Nigel Kneale's *The Stone Tape* (1972) for TV, and Shirley Jackson's 1959 classic *The Haunting of Hill House*.

These ghostly tropes – a sense of temporal disjunction, fragments, found and missing objects, the steady erosion of hitherto unassailable 'truths', intrusions from the past into the present via the future where ghosts and spirits 'wait' for the living, 'remnants of the past which refuse to be domesticated and which return, repeatedly' (Coverley, 2020, p.94) – open the way to an understanding of hauntology in thought and praxis. Having established some of the basics, let us now return to the philosophical basis for hauntology.

2.1 Derridean Hauntology

> Let us not begin at the beginning . . .
>
> – Jacques Derrida, *Archive Fever*[5]

Derrida is best known as one of the most important figures in the development of philosophical deconstruction, which is situated within the fields of post-structuralism, postmodernism and literary theory. A little introductory background on Derrida's deconstructive thinking will help to place hauntology in its wider philosophical and artistic landscape. Deconstruction is a somewhat slippery concept, but, in brief, it aims to challenge and probe metaphysical binary oppositions by exploring areas of aporia within the Western metaphysical philosophical tradition. Derrida's texts frequently engage with earlier philosophical thinkers, such as Plato, Husserl, Heidegger, Hegel and Marx, as well as artists and scientists including Valerio Adami and Freud, which he uses to explore and confront a series of interlinked conceptions relating to the centre, the archive, *pharmakoi*[6] and other areas of undecidability, including hauntology.

Derrida was always wary of thinking of deconstruction as a 'method' or means of analysis, instead preferring to locate it within an ever-developing field of possibilities, pertaining to invention, experience and understanding in the broadest sense. As a field, deconstruction was always expected to evolve, with Derrida noting: 'If the foundations are assured, there is no construction: neither is there any invention' (Brunette & Wills, 1994, p.27), and 'if it were an identifiable and regulated practice, the same thing being recognized each time, then it would not have a chance. It would be stillborn, dead from the start' (Brunette & Wills, 1994, p.28). But is deconstruction really applicable to fields outside writing and philosophy, Derrida's principal foci of enquiry? Derrida comments:

> I would say that the idea that deconstruction should confine itself to the analysis of the discursive text – I know that the idea is widespread – is really either a gross misunderstanding or a political strategy designed to limit deconstruction to matters of language. Deconstruction starts with the deconstruction of logocentrism, and thus to want to confine it to linguistic phenomena is the most suspect of operations. (Brunette & Wills, 1994, p.15)

Furthermore, Derrida contends that the surface that carries the text, whether physical or spectral 'paper', also carries within it a much larger and more

---

[5] Derrida, 1996, p.1.
[6] First discussed by Derrida in 'Plato's Pharmacy', *pharmakoi* embody undecidability, occupying dual states simultaneously (poison/medicine, first/last), resisting conceptual order through their originary ambivalence and untranslatability.

complex field of performative actions pertaining to sound, voice and body (Derrida, 2005, p.44):

> Paper echoes and resounds, *subjectile* of an inscription from which phonetic aspects are never absent, whatever the system of writing. Beneath the appearance of a surface, it holds in reserve a volume, folds, a labyrinth whose walls return the echoes of the voice or song that it carries itself; for paper also has the range or the ranges of a voice bearer. (Derrida, 2005 [italic in the original])

This description is apt for tape and records, fundamental constituents of hauntological music of the twenty-first century and earlier. Physical recordings, like paper, 'hold in reserve a volume' of echoes, deeply embedded in their grooves of inscription. Thus, according to Derrida, from its very foundation onwards, any field or object of enquiry is open to deconstruction – indeed *should* be deconstructed – without which the alternatives are stagnation, ossification and the death of invention. Deconstructive approaches to diverse domains, such as theatre, film, architecture, music, law and the visual arts, are now commonplace within the academy and further afield.

But what exactly – or inexactly – is hauntology, which in much contemporary music practice appears to condense around a certain 'atmosphere' that is enabled by the importation of analogue technology into an often, but not necessarily, digital soundscape? To begin to answer this question, we must consider Derrida's original conception of hauntology, and then examine how the term's practical and theoretical usage has developed during the last three decades. Of course, whenever Derrida is brought into a conversation, the idea of a 'beginning' is a vexed one. Put simply, origins and centres are highly questionable; everything is coming *from* somewhere and going somewhere *else*, conceptually, linguistically, temporally and even physically in some instances, and this restless portability is nicely encapsulated by recorded music, in particular by analogue's physical 'housings' of tapes and records. To observe the coalescing of Derrida's neologism, we must return to the 1990s and *Specters of Marx: The State of the Debt, the Work of Mourning and the New International* (1996, p.1), Derrida's extended musings on Marx, Marxism, history and lost futures.

A certain evolutionary quality – in that the ways in which we understand and use words changes according to their contexts, times and users – is central to contemporary understandings of Derrida's neologism. The unstable developmental nature of meaning and usage aligns with and amplifies other deconstructive tenets of course, for it throws questions of authors, origins and centres into doubt, while also allowing for the permanent deferment of the arrival of a fully stable meaning or use, generating potentially endless hermeneutic permutations.[7] The word *hauntology* – derived from the French *hantologie* and *ontologie* – plays through contexts of difference, differences that can be read but not always heard, written but not *effectively* spoken; hauntology is thus caught up in the same net as *différance*, another of Derrida's neologisms. As Wortham (2010, p.36) notes: '*différance* is a . . . neologism coined by Derrida to establish the limits of phonocentrism. *Différance* combines and develops a sense of differing and deferral implied by the French word "*différence*"'. Wortham suggests that 'Derrida frequently includes *différance* in an unmasterable chain or untitleable series that also includes the trace, the supplement, the remainder, writing, dissemination, pharmakon, cinder and so on' (Wortham, 2010, p.37 [italic in the original]). Thus, although one of *différance*'s key attributes is what might be loosely termed its speech-curtailing properties, it is its capacity for an implied *deferral* that is of most relevance here. In French, the full play of *différance* is evident in the two spellings of *hantologie* and *ontologie*, which have an *almost* identical pronunciation.

Considering hauntology's almost omnipresence in contemporary cultural usage, its first appearance in *Specters of Marx* occurs with little fanfare. Appearing just three times in the entire text, as a term, it is far from central to the main thesis – unlike 'specter', whose appearances are numerous throughout. The word 'hauntology' first appears when Derrida poses the question '*What* is a ghost?'

> Repetition *and* first time: this is perhaps the question of the event as question of the ghost. *What is* a ghost? What is the *effectivity* or the *presence* of a specter, that is, of what seems to remain as ineffective, virtual, insubstantial as a simulacrum? Is there *there*, between the thing itself and its simulacrum, an opposition that holds up? Repetition *and* first time, but also repetition *and* last time. Each time it is the event itself, a first time is a last time. Altogether other. Staging for the end of history. Let us call it a *hauntology*. (Derrida, 2006, p.10 [italic in the original])

Derrida poses his ghostly question as though a series of riddles, presenting the ghost/event as unsettling temporal order, emerging from the past to haunt the present, yet also provoking apprehension in the *future* of its impending *return*, while this event/ghost is also capable of overturning spatial order – its presence – as Derrida questions the *there* between event and simulacrum. The first *and* last time of each manifestation defies conceptual order by coexisting in an endless movable chain of repetition and opposition, in a similar way to the supplement and the drug/poison of the *pharmakon*. It's also worth considering that Derrida's choice of the word 'staging' covertly implies the performative repetition of the supplement, an apt treatment for the theatrical housing of Hamlet's ghost.

---

[7] A Google search in 2024 offers over 2 million results for the term.

The second appearance occurs during an analysis of the 'conjuration' against Marxism:

> this frontier between the public and the private is constantly being displaced, remaining less assured than ever . . . because the medium in which it is instituted, namely, the medium of the media themselves (news, the press, telecommunications, techno-tele-discursivity, techno-tele-iconicity . . .), this element itself is neither living nor dead, present nor absent: it spectralizes. It does not belong to ontology . . . or to the essence of life or death. It requires, then . . . *hauntology*. We will take this category to be irreducible, and first of all to everything it makes possible: ontology, theology, positive or negative onto-theology. (Derrida, 2006, p.63 [italic in the original])

Moving from ghostly ontology in the first quotation, Derrida now attaches 'hauntology' to a discussion of the 'medium of the media', especially where it concerns technology (the 'techno') – technology that contracts both *space* ('tele', meaning far or distant) and *time*. By adding 'iconicity' to his portmanteau word, Derrida draws in the concept of a word (or thing) that can refer beyond itself – its hidden 'ghosts' – while 'discursivity' implies not only an expansive use of language per se, but also the collection of accepted or hegemonic norms from a particular period, all at the service of the 'techno-tele'. The movement of decentring continues, challenging fixed concepts of public/private, life/death and presence/absence, while also resisting reduction to a central fixed category. Hauntology overturns these conceptual oppositions, and Derrida's use of neither/nor in this passage further emphasises this point. Of course, this is not new territory for Derrida: in 'Plato's Pharmacy' (2004, pp.119–22) he uses the *pharmakon*'s qualities of 'either/or', 'neither/nor' 'and' paradox as a strategy to probe similar concerns more than twenty years before the publication of *Specters of Marx*. It is also worth noting just how well Derrida's unfolding explication of hauntology aligns with the virtuality, one might even say 'ghostliness', of capital – that is to say, capital's operation through promissory notes rather than barter or exchange, its status as revenant, passing from hand to hand, with each transaction part of an endlessly repeating 'first and last', it's lack of traceability and its virtuality, present long before cryptocurrencies came into vogue.

Derrida's third and final mention of hauntology occurs as an amplification of the undecidability already hinted at in the second quotation and the nature, or logic, of the ghost found in the earlier quotation. However, in the third instance, Derrida has vastly expanded the term's field of operation:

> To haunt does not mean to be present, and it is necessary to introduce haunting into the very construction of a concept. Of every concept, beginning with the concepts of being and time. That is what we would be calling here

> a hauntology. Ontology opposes it only in a movement of exorcism. Ontology is a conjuration. (Derrida, 2006, p.202)

Hauntology 'has now come to reside within every concept, and its presence can be felt everywhere and in every time' (Coverley, 2020, p.210). Hauntology no longer needs italicisation as an 'outsider' or 'foreign' import, for it is now an established part of the discourse, taking its place with ontology, theology, onto-theology and so on. This final passage also reaffirms the spatial (and temporal) undecidability of hauntology – 'it does not mean to be present' – but also confirms its status as an agent of temporal decentring, permeating being and time. In many ways, this returns to the domain of the *pharmakon*, not only as regards undecidability but also in the use of words that are closely aligned to the *pharmakon* (*pharmakos/pharmakeus*); that is, we return 'into the very construction of a concept', the différance of *pharmakos/pharmakeus, hantologie/ontologie*, with the clue to the *pharmakon* comprising Derrida's use of the word 'conjure' in conjunction with ontology, which immediately draws the text into the orbit of the scapegoat (*pharmakos*) and the *pharmakeus*, the Derridean sorcerer of 'Plato's Pharmacy', both of whom occupy liminal spaces at the edges of society. Both are simultaneously within and without that society. This passage also brings into play the exorcism: as idea, as ritual, as return and as promise. Additionally, it appears to confirm ontology's coexistence with hauntology, if it is only through the act of exorcism that ontology *opposes* hauntology. An exorcism of what, though? In *Specters of Marx*, it might be an exorcism of 'what may be' or 'what has been', an exorcism of future possibility and past/present memory, an exorcism of the 'undead' (ghosts) rather than the dead, or any combination thereof. Would a post-exorcism world exist in a state of eternal 'present' or is ontology itself an exorcism, ridding the 'now' of both memory and hope through the 'magically' enabled return to conceptual order delivered by the sorcerer (*pharmakeus*)?

Associated with the concept of repetition, and in particular to its *pharmakon*-like qualities of first/last time, haunting is present in the construction of every concept, haunting is present in hauntology, and time being 'out of joint' is a theme that is woven into the fabric of much of Derrida's work (not just *Specters of Marx*).[8] Also, if 'it is necessary to introduce haunting into the very construction of a concept' then the implication is that haunting would *precede* every concept, and that hauntology itself must be haunted by the ghosts of repetition. Origins and centres are no longer assured; they are unstable, always already *there* and yet in no fixed time or place. Thus, *Specters* establishes three key areas of initial hauntological problematicity: ontologies of the

---

[8] *Archive Fever* (1998), *The Work of Mourning* (2001) and *Cinders* (2014) explore this concept.

Cage, Nono and 1960s Hauntology 11

ghostly, the virtual (and therefore spatial) and the spatio-temporal, which are evident across a broad range of subject approaches in twenty-first-century writing about Derridean hauntology.

These areas of concern can be further refined in praxis:

- Decentring – time, space, presence, absence, ghosts and spectres (supplement and *pharmakon*) as embodied by musical technology.
- Repetition – the placing of first/last time within an endless thread of past/future possibilities, present in modern recording techniques and much mid-century (tape) compositional practice.
- Virtuality and the 'medium of the media' – including television, online streaming, CDs, radio, records, tape and print news.

Music and media have a long shared history, from concert reviews and interviews being a frequent component of print media from the eighteenth century onwards, followed by the introduction of mass participation through radio – often via the broadcasting of records and tape recordings – the concomitant rise of the DJ and later transference to television media, to the twenty-first century's 'live' streaming revolution on platforms such as YouTube and TikTok, especially during the 2020s COVID pandemic global lockdowns. Derrida's emphasis on the word 'medium' raises further questions of 'what' exactly we are listening to, the performance or the medium itself? Crackles, pops, hiss and jumps foreground analogue media, while compression does the same for the digital. This question will come to dominate more recent developments in musical hauntology.

The decentring of time and space is easily mapped to any form of portable media. Recorded music allows us to endlessly share in a time and a place that is past and (usually) geographically distant, often engaging with both performers and composers who are already dead – they speak to us, but they cannot answer. Likewise, the musical 'score' is a blueprint for future performances, mute until activated through practice. The score also opens up the possibility of endless repetition within an unmasterable chain of 'unique' events. Every performance is first *and* last, even when we have a favourite recording on loop. This applies equally to live performance as to recordings, or where the two are combined, as can be heard in Cage's *33⅓* and Nono's *La fabbrica illuminata*. Finally, it can be mapped to the medium of the media: because the media's principal function historically has been to convey 'news', it invariably decentres time and space – we see, listen to, or read reportage from an incident that happened yesterday, or five minutes ago, in a city halfway across the world. Very rarely are we at the centre of that reportage: tiny delays in dissemination make the truly 'live' and simultaneous broadcast a virtual impossibility. Since World War II, music recordings, including tape and record – unless they document a 'live' event – are mostly composed from myriad fragments, with individual takes occupying a much-expanded timeframe to a live performance; and parts may not even be recorded simultaneously, either temporally or spatially. Thus, the majority of musical sound documents – across all genres – represent a very different creative and aural experience for performers and listeners than a live concert would, in a process that releases both composers and performers from the constraints of narrative 'concert' time and place.

2.2 The Play of Hauntology: Crate Digging, Lost Futures and Radical Atheism

... the spirit of *reverent* exploitation ...
— Simon Reynolds, *Retromania*[9]

Aligned with the spectral, in which the word *hauntology* is inextricably entangled, another of *Specters of Marx*'s recurring temporal tropes is based around a quotation from Shakespeare's *Hamlet* (act 1, scene 5, line 188), 'The time is out of joint', from which Derrida weaves a complex net of linking ideas of political economy, Marx's legacy, Marxism's legacy, time, space, inheritance, spectres, spirits and mourning. As a construct, hauntology required an appropriate context to facilitate its assemblage (the ghostly orbit of *Specters of Marx*); but as Derrida (2006, p.xvi) says, 'a context, always, remains open, thus fallible and insufficient', opening the door for further expansion in practice. As the Google search figure confirms, hauntology is well and truly established in the cultural lexicon currently in operation; virus-like, hauntology has seeped into much contemporary cultural discourse, from literature, music and the visual arts to broader philosophical-historical areas such as ruins studies, Anthropocene studies and posthumanism. The growth of other spectrality studies also coincides with revived academic (and wider) interests in the ghostly. Indeed, hauntology is such common currency now that an author such as David Cecchetto (2013, p.14) can refer to a chapter as 'conduct[ing] a hauntology of the positivist definition of life that Dyens extrapolates from Dawkins' without actually referencing hauntology again in the main body of his text: thus, hauntology has added a system of critique to its other meanings.

Much twenty-first-century musical usage of the term has emphasised either lost futures or the (invariably electronic) sonic identity of hauntology – most frequently signified through the sound of the medium itself, either through wear and tear, or as a blank, a sonic 'absence' – in the work of various artists and subgenres, obvious examples including Ghost Box records, Aphex Twin,

---

[9] Reynolds, 2011, p.323, emphasis adjusted.

Burial, the Caretaker, William Basinski, Christian Marclay, hauntological pop, hypnagogic pop, glo-fi and chillwave. As explicated in the writings of Simon Reynolds and Mark Fisher et al., this brings hauntology right back into the technological realm, to Derrida's 'techno-tele-iconicity' and the dissemination of technologically recorded archives as symptomatic of 'an ache of longing – for history itself' (Reynolds, 2011, p.356).

'Consummate scavengers, the hauntologists trawl through charity shops, street markets and jumble sales for delectable morsels of decaying culture-matter' (Reynolds, 2011, p.328). Simon Reynolds's *Retromania* (2011) brings hauntology into the twenty-first century, placing its focus firmly on late twentieth- and early twenty-first-century pop music's obsession with recycling its recent past, creating music subgenres dominated by repetition (sampling and looping), nostalgia (children's TV), lost futures (the UK welfare state, modernist creative practice), ghosts and the spectral, abstract noise (prog and psychedelia), decay and analogue techniques, instruments and media, mainly placed within a timeframe of the 1950s–80s. Recycle, retro, reuse, return, revenant, revolution . . . hauntology is the ology that just can't let go, and through what we might term 'haunted' media – including radio – decay has been foregrounded across musical and material domains. Of course, noughties popular music is far from the first to use such processes of foregrounding; John Lennon's 'Revolution 9' from the Beatles' *White Album* (1968) is a collage of numerous 'scavenged' and overlaid recorded sound fragments, while the opening of Pink Floyd's 'Wish You Were Here' (*Wish You Were Here*, 1975) utilises radio static and fragments of programmes – recorded from David Gilmour's car radio – as a prelude to the opening guitar chords of the song. Floyd also evoked early NASA radio transmissions in 'Astronomy Domine' (*The Piper at the Gates of Dawn*, 1967), although the effect was actually created by reading planets' names through a megaphone. Similar earlier processes of overwriting are prevalent in dub music, where remixes of samples and existing tracks heavily manipulate vocal and rhythmic content, as exemplified by Lee 'Scratch' Perry (his 1968 single 'People Funny Boy' includes rhythmised samples of a crying baby), while hip hop's love of sampling combined with the foregrounding of the sounds of vinyl, tape and radio as media themselves – their crackle, pop, hiss and static – also foreshadows hauntological music's sonic lexicon.

For Reynolds (2011, p.335), 'hauntology is all about memory's power (to linger, pop up unbidden, prey on your mind) and memory's fragility (destined to become distorted, to fade, then finally disappear)'. The mass of currently freely available recorded sonic detritus of earlier decades is the ideal starting point for this focus, with recordings acting as the ghostly aides-memoires to what has gone before (and *where* it has gone) even though they can still be accessed in the 'now', thereby contracting both time *and* space. The flipside to documenting era-specific cultural objects before they are lost[10] – as a process of preservation – is the importance of documenting processes of decay also, in what Reynolds (2011, p.336) describes as 'the foredoomed nature of recording's attempts at cultural embalming', while the potential for damage caused during the storage and retrieval of sonic and visual documents is an important tool in hauntological music, layering nostalgia and loss as symptomatic of a yearning for lost futures and the stabilising power of history itself. As is amply demonstrated in the work of the Caretaker and Position Normal,[11] the feelings of nostalgia and lost futures associated with memory as a concept make it a powerful creative stimulus, especially when it has been fractured by conditions such as Alzheimer's disease, where the gradual erosion of the ability to retain memories of new events nullifies the present, leaving only the ghostly remains of the past, their histories played out through multiple layers of sampling. However, musical hauntologists do not have to restrict themselves to shellac, vinyl and tape to create the 'crumbly smudges' and 'wavering, mottled quality' of the antique (Reynolds, 2011, pp.331–32). As well as utilising vintage equipment (synthesisers, oscillators, tape decks and other analogue technology) as playback and creative tools, creating a deliberately 'retro' sound, antiquated sonorities can also be recreated through contemporary digital processes – masquerading as analogue sources – or by processing original analogue sources digitally, both creative approaches being reminiscent of W. G. Sebald's photocopied 'vintage' images in *The Rings of Saturn*.[12]

'Conjecture: hauntology has an intrinsically sonic dimension' (Fisher, 2014, p.120). Using the term 'hauntology' to describe various popular music genres around the same time as Reynolds,[13] Mark Fisher (1968–2017) brought a further updated understanding and usage of the concept to a considerably wider audience than Derrida's original had ever achieved. As Derrida had emphasised the *tele* of

---

[10] There are many examples of TV programmes that had been lost being restored to a broadcaster's archive decades later through viewer's home recordings and 'bootleg' versions, with resulting quality loss as a natural consequence. The BBC (UK) maintained a policy of wiping and reusing tapes from the 1960s to the 1980s, resulting in the loss of many episodes of, for example, *Doctor Who* (series 1 and 2), now considered to be classics of the genre. For more information, see www.mentalfloss.com/article/501607/wipe-out-when-bbc-kept-erasing-its-own-history. It's also worth reflecting upon Fisher's (2014, p.2) contention that 'in conditions of digital recall, loss itself is lost'.

[11] James Leyland Kirby's alter ego the Caretaker, named after the eponymous character in *The Shining*, was active from 1999 to 2019. Chris Bailiff and John Cushway's duo Position Normal has been active since 1986. Both deploy extensive use of vintage samples to evoke memory and nostalgia in their music.

[12] Sebald recopied contemporary photographs until the images became so blurred they took on the qualities of damaged early photographic prints. For more information, see Grant Gee's documentary *Patience (After Sebald): A Walk Through the Rings of Saturn* (2012).

[13] Reynolds remarks: 'Enter hauntology, a term that critic Mark Fisher and I started bandying around in 2005 to describe a loose network of mostly UK artists' (Reynolds, 2011, p.328).

technology, in both temporal and spatial terms, and the weight of loss, inheritance and mourning in *Specters of Marx*, Fisher developed these aspects of Derrida's thought in assorted writings on his *k-punk* blog and subsequent book publication (Fisher, 2018) and in the book *Ghosts of My Life: Writings on Depression, Hauntology and Lost Futures* (2014), developing hauntology's usage in a new context with another parallel, and supplemental, interpretation. Thus, in a sense, hauntology itself was already generating ghosts, coming back to haunt *Specters of Marx* from the future as a revenant, crossing between texts and media, shaping content through context[14] and entering the virtual in the realms of music, electronic communication, film and video.

I think it is worth pausing for a moment here to look at the word 'haunting', as its fluidity of usage forms an important part of its application to music. The title *Ghosts of My Life* appears to indicate a much more personal dimension to hauntology than in Reynolds's discourse, where haunting and loss dominate. 'Haunting' is a slippery word, no doubt one of the reasons that it attracted Derrida in the first place. There is 'haunt' as place of *return*, for example, the 'haunt of musicians' referring to a particular locus, such as an after-concert meeting place. There is more abstract usage, such as 'the haunt of lost souls', indicating an imaginary – or possibly virtual – domain, while there is also 'haunting' as memory, a haunting strain of music, or scent, or taste. Then there is haunting as the act of a ghost or spectre, as can be read in the English translation of Marx and Engels's 1848 *Manifesto of the Communist Party*, 'a spectre is haunting Europe – the spectre of Communism' (1985, p.78); but, as Derrida comments in *Specters of Marx*, when Marx wrote the manifesto communism as a modern political movement had not come into being. Thus the spectre can apparently haunt *from* the future, as well as embody the memories of past events or people and the apprehension of their *return*. Derrida (2006, p.10) sums up this temporal and spatial paradox when he asks, 'What does it mean to follow a ghost? And what if this came down to being followed by it . . . persecuted perhaps by the very chase we are leading? . . . what seems to be out front, the future, comes back in advance: from the past, from the back', thereby underlining the impossibility for Derrida of any originary signification in the construction of a concept, including ontology.

It is somewhat ironic that Fisher was not a natural acolyte of Derrida, finding his circumlocutions intensely irritating, and noting:

> I'd generally found Jacques Derrida . . . a frustrating thinker. . . . Deconstruction was a kind of pathology of scepticism, which induced

---

[14] What Derrida (2006, p.63) describes as a 'performative interpretation, that is, of an interpretation that transforms the very thing it interprets'.

> hedging, infirmity of purpose and compulsory doubt in its followers. It elevated particular modes of academic practice – Heidegger's priestly opacity, literary theory's emphasis on the ultimate instability of any interpretation – into quasi-theological imperatives. (Fisher, 2014, pp.16–17)

For this reason, it is perhaps unsurprising that Fisher chose to draw more inspiration from authors other than Derrida, most notably the Swedish philosopher Martin Hägglund. Fisher (2014, p.17) introduces hauntology as 'this concept, or puncept. The pun was on the philosophical concept of ontology, the philosophical study of what can be said to exist', before continuing his examination of Derridean hauntological forerunners, such as the trace and différance, the main difference being hauntology's engagement with the subject of time, most notably that of time that is 'out of joint'. Fisher considers hauntology further through Hägglund's *Radical Atheism: Derrida and the Time of Life*, particularly Hägglund's (2008, p.82) assertion of the importance of the ghost's relationality to '*the no longer or not yet*'. In *Radical Atheism*, Hägglund argues that, contrary to the readings of other commentators – such as John D. Caputo – Derrida never embraced an 'ethical or religious "turn" in [his] thinking' instead arguing that 'a radical atheism informs his writing from beginning to end' (Hägglund, 2008, p.1). Taking Derrida's engagement with time as a starting point, Hägglund develops this line of enquiry further, bringing Derrida's work on ethics, desire, justice and identity into his reading. Although much of Hägglund's text does not directly concern pop culture, which Fisher explicates in *Ghosts of My Life*, Derrida's three mentions of hauntology in *Specters of Marx* are of considerable importance to Fisher's interpretation, and for this reason, I think it is worth examining them in more detail. The first deals with ghosts, societal demarcation and economies of violence:

> Derrida's aim is to formulate a general 'hauntology' (*hantologie*), in contrast to the traditional 'ontology' that thinks being in terms of self-identical presence. What is important about the figure of the specter, then, is that it cannot be fully present: it has no being in itself but marks a relation to what is *no longer* or *not yet*. And since time – the disjointure between past and future – is a condition even for the slightest moment, spectrality is at work in everything that happens. (Hägglund, 2008, p.82 [italic in the original])

In the second occurrence, Hägglund says:

> At several places in *Specters of Marx* he [Derrida] maintains that a completely present life – which would not be 'out of joint', not haunted by any ghosts – would be nothing but a complete death. . . . In a state of being where all violent change is precluded, nothing can ever happen. (Hägglund, 2008, p.84 [italic in the original])

The final deliberation puts hauntology into conversation with notions of justice:

> If life were fully present itself, if it were not haunted by what has been lost in the past and what may be lost in the future, there would be nothing that could cause the concern for justice.... There can be no justice without a memory of what is *no longer* that is kept for a future that is *not yet*. (Hägglund, 2008, p.140 [italic in the original])

Taking these three passages together, Hägglund argues for relationality between a past that is lost and a future that is still to come, personified through the figure of the spectre. Because of this relationality, the spectre (as part of hauntology) is a consistent presence, and without the spectre, humanity would exist in an endless and ossified 'present' – echoing Francis Fukuyama's liberal capitalist eschatology (see Fukuyama, 1992). Peace can only exist if it is simultaneously accompanied by the agent of change that is violence; and without the presence of past and future spectres (as regret/loss and hope), there can be no justice.

Fisher is particularly interested in hauntology's reference to both the remnants of the past – often physical – and their associated memories, with a yearning for 'lost futures'; so hauntology is

> that which is (in actuality is) *no longer*, but which *remains* effective as a virtuality (the traumatic 'compulsion to repeat', a fatal pattern). The second sense of hauntology refers to that which (in actuality) has *not yet* happened, but which is *already* effective in the virtual (an attractor, an anticipation shaping current behaviour). (Fisher, 2014, p.19 [italic in the original])

Fisher proceeds to consider the importance of hauntology as 'materialised memory' (Fisher, 2014, p.21), emphasising the tactile material dimension of specifically analogue media, their use in music and their degradation and breakdown, which further accentuates the revenant's ability to conjure up not only memories of 'things' (often distorted) but also memories of things that never were, an insatiable and melancholy longing for what *did not* come to pass – what Derrida (2006, p.113) calls the 'heirs ... of a promise'. Vinyl 'crackle', the hiss of degrading tape[15] and so on are not only representative of decaying past (and tactile) media; these sounds also foreground the *media* themselves, through their imperfections, all the while opening new sonic avenues where 'loss' is the driving force of creation.[16] Similar preoccupations can be observed in the visual arts, with artists such as Angela Chalmers and Chloe McCarrick interrogating women's

---

[15] Decaying tape hiss was the basis for William Basinski's *The Disintegration Loops* (2001). Basinski notes: 'the iron oxide particles were gradually turning to dust and dropping into the tape machine, leaving bare plastic spots on the tape, and silence in these corresponding sections of the new recording' (Reynolds, 2011, p.336).

[16] Also referencing sonic arts' standard usage of hauntology as 'crackle'.

histories and the detritus of pop culture using the vintage photographic technique of the cyanotype,[17] while Walead Beshty used the same technique in his monumental 2014 exhibition[18] at the Curve Gallery at London's Barbican Centre, where he created more than twelve thousand cyanotypes. The cyanotypes were printed on the cellulose-based remains of exhibition-related social interactions (printed letters, contracts and emails) and other waste (paper, card and wood), while additionally depicting the studio and exhibition space and its activities, thereby opening up the *processes* of history (and artistic production) to the viewer and the meanings of objects that are no longer considered of financial or historical worth. As Derrida (2006, p.67) remarks, 'like all inheritors, we are in mourning', ... even when all we inherit is a 'lost' future.

Similar preoccupations that combine acts of memorialisation and loss with the ecological impact of the 'throw-away society' are evident in music, with the turntablist Christian Marclay (b. 1955) observing: 'When there is excess, when there are thrift stores filled with books and records that are 25 cents apiece, it makes you think about objects differently' (Gordon & Marclay, 2005, p.19). Thus, the revenant becomes synonymous with reuse in this context. The endless 'scavenging' (as Reynolds puts it) of earlier material has hauntological implications for the current climate emergency, whereby, for example, oil-derived 'plastic' media (tape, LPs and radio sets) act as both the tactile, decaying ghosts of vintage means of production and dissemination, while also hinting at what 'has *not yet* happened, but which is *already* effective in the virtual' – the impending climate disaster that is looming as a direct consequence of humanity's overexploitation of natural planetary resources in the seemingly unquenchable desire for more possessions demanded by capitalism. Although often associated with the 1990s and early noughties, terms such as plunderphonics, crate digging and sampladelic, which describe various methods of creative recycling in music, resonate strongly with the current climate-crisis driven mantra of 'reduce, reuse, recycle'. They have profound implications for the vexed relationship between music and capital, problematising issues of production and reception, ownership and authorship and access and decentring. They also echo many of the tenets of earlier movements in the visual arts, especially Arte Povera – the 1960s–70s radical Italian movement that embraced the usage of non-traditional and waste materials as both reflecting Italian economic instability and attempting to

---

[17] Cyanotypes are one of the simplest and oldest types of photography, using two chemicals plus water to develop cyan blue monochrome prints.

[18] Walead Beshty, *A Partial Disassembling of an Invention Without a Future: Helter-Skelter and Random Notes in which the Pulleys and Cogwheels are Lying Around at Random All Over the Workbench*, Barbican Centre, London, 2014. See www.regenprojects.com/artists/waleadbeshty/biography.

confront the capitalist model of the art gallery, represented by Piero Manzoni and Michelangelo Pistoletto among others – and Japan's Mono-ha (school of things) movement, whose members included Jiro Takamatsu and Lee Ufan. Mono-ha's rejection of traditional practices during the 1960s and later, replaced by a focus on the nature of raw materials, was used to challenge contemporary rampant Japanese industrialisation. Two musician-creators who encapsulate these concerns are Christian Marclay and the Caretaker. Marclay's interdisciplinary work has consistently championed using materials for their own sake, while also challenging the industrial 'culture machine'. Describing his museum works as 'these flea-market-like installations' (Sherburne & Marclay, 2014, p.49), Marclay's many creations for found objects (CDs, records, tape, photographs and video), such as *Record Without a Cover* (1985) and *Shake, Rattle and Roll (fluxmix)* (2004), problematise the ownership, *bricolage* and decay of physical materials, while the Caretaker's obsession with 'tomb-raiding pop's cemetery, defiling the corpses' (Reynolds, 2011, p.355) sees the reuse of abandoned physical sound documents in pieces as varied as *Selected Memories from the Haunted Ballroom* (1999) and *Extra Patience (After Sebald)* (2012). Both artists either implicitly or explicitly emphasise the possibilities for 'short-circuiting' capitalism's circulatory processes through networks of shared micro-autonomy.

Capitalism's grip on early twenty-first-century culture was an important theme for Fisher, having already covered related ground in his *Capitalist Realism* (2009). In *Ghosts*, he raises the point that 'the era of what I have called "capitalist realism" – the widespread belief that there is no alternative to capitalism – has been haunted not by the apparition of the spectre of communism, but by its disappearance' (Fisher, 2014, p.19), and uses the example of the exponential growth of cyberspace during the late twentieth and early twenty-first century as the means of 'reception, distribution and consumption of culture – especially music culture' (Fisher, 2014, p.20) as a fundamental part of this process. And yet, this virtual hauntological domain, contracting space and time, haunting from past and future, is what has allowed hauntological artists to converge in what Fisher (2014, p.21) calls 'an existential orientation' and where, despite the apparent collapse of hope engendered by the disintegration of post-war modernist ideals, 'the music constitutes a refusal to give up on the desire for the future'[19] providing 'a political dimension, because it amounts to a failure to accommodate to the closed horizons of capitalist realism'. And this is one of the ways that hauntology, through vintage media technologies, is

---

[19] Those who lived through this era (c. 1950–80) were exposed to the possibilities of what are now 'lost futures' through avenues of popular culture – film, television and various music genres – where modernist ideals and futurology saturated the currency of the everyday.

a *radical* form of decentring: it uses one of capitalism's main avenues of commerce, the Internet, against capitalism, instead using cyberspace to create – through digital audio workstations (DAWs) and other digital technologies – and disseminate artistic products that are created through processes of bricolage and reassemblage from the discarded remains of previous eras, often acquired for little money or for free. Much of this work is also disseminated directly by the artists or through wider artists' collectives, thereby eliminating the 'middleman' of the twentieth-century record company in a similar way to Arte Povera's fight against the traditional gallery system. If free access to creative outputs is also available – via YouTube, UbuWeb and so on – then that radicality is increased, as the circle of exchange denies capital as an external force. However, Coverley makes an interesting counterpoint, arguing that Fisher (and Derrida) along with other left-leaning commentators, are blind to, what might be termed, the hauntology of the right:

> Politically . . . hauntology remains uniformly wedded to the political left. Indeed, if there is a blind spot . . . in Derrida and Fisher's articulation of hauntology, it is a seeming lack of awareness that the ghosts, spectres and revenants of an earlier age may invoke a quite different politics to that espoused by those on the left and one not necessarily of our choosing. . . . It seems to me that rather than spectres of Marx . . . the prevailing spirit of the last 30 years in the UK is one which has been conjured from . . . Thatcherism. (Coverley, 2020, pp.268–69)

Although few would argue with Coverley concerning domestic UK politics, I wonder whether this is actually true when it comes to music and the arts. Is there a creative hauntology of the right? What of Fashwave, whose use of appropriated '80s synth sounds combined with a visual style of imperialist tropes, encompassing everything from Roman gladiators to Nazi knick-knacks, feeds into the alt-right's current political narratives?[20] As both Fisher and Derrida state clearly that Marx and Marxism(s) are dead in the capitalist realist state of politics that the early twenty-first century finds itself enmeshed in, I am not sure whether it is as much of a blind spot as Coverley suggests. Fisher (2014, p.28) acknowledges the possibility for a more negative political tone in hauntology further when he explains: 'There is the specific sense in which it [hauntology] has been applied to music culture, and a more general sense, where it refers to persistences, repetitions, prefigurations. There are also more or *less benign* versions' (my italics). Both the decline of twentieth-century music culture's role in imagining futures that are now lost and hauntological

---

[20] www.theguardian.com/music/musicblog/2016/dec/14/fashwave-synth-music-co-opted-by-the-far-right.

music's signalling of the decline of these popular modernist ideals is placed alongside analyses of varying states of symptomatic nostalgia and melancholia, and what Fisher (2014, p.25) sees as the false dehistoricising narrative of populist PR in the twenty-first century that asserts that 'intensity and innovation are equally distributed throughout all cultural periods'.

2.3 Hauntology and Other Fields

Thus, developing Derrida's initial remarks, Fisher et al. took hauntology from the nineteenth to the twenty-first century, emphasising the queasy sense of dyschronia in late twentieth-century popular culture and millennial music, while bringing politics into the centre of their discourses. Unlike Derrida, who takes a decidedly non-Marxist view of Marx's legacy – it was never his intention to present a new Marxist manifesto – Fisher is happy to place the blame for the exponential growth in nostalgia, symptomatic of wider cultural decline, firmly at the doorsteps of neoliberalism and the final death of the counter-culture's revolutionary ideals towards the end of 1970s. Thus, raking through the recorded detritus of the near past and endlessly repeating it across other formats, coupled with the melancholy of futures that appeared bright with hope – politically, culturally and socially – but that never materialised, are key concepts necessary to an understanding of post-Derridean hauntology. Not that hauntology is confined to popular music culture. Representative views from other fields, many of which draw on Fisher and Reynolds work, reference similar foci, such as: 'hauntology contrasts the spirit or essence of a thing with its countless materializations or specters, which allow for the persistence of spirit as memory' (Banita, 2010, p.97); 'the concept [hauntology] allowed Derrida to use the philosophically problematic figure of the ghost – neither being nor non-being, both presence and absence simultaneously – to discuss the uncanny persistence of Marx's ideas after the death of communism' (Reynolds, 2011, pp.328–29); 'the inscription of multiple temporalities within the time-image coincides remarkably with Derrida's description of the effect of the *chose*, the thing called specter: "It desynchronizes, it recalls us to anachrony"' (Cuntz, 2010, p.119) and hauntology as 'the idea that originary signification is an ontological impossibility because all meaning is informed, overshadowed and haunted by the ghosts of other meanings' (Van Elferen, 2010, p.287). Persistence, repetition, ghosts, revenants, dyschronia and what Coverley calls the 'technological uncanny' (Coverley, 2020, p.15) all feature prominently in millennial and postmillennial definitions, but what of earlier manifestations? Is there an equally political 'pre-hauntological' hauntology, groaning under the weight of its own – recently – recorded past, from earlier in the twentieth century?

'The whole performance was a montage of authentic speeches, essays, newspaper cuttings, appeals, pamphlets, photographs, and film of the War and the Revolution, of historical persons and scenes' (Piscator, 1980, p.94). Although this description could apply to a post-war multimedia opera, such as B.A. Zimmermann's *Die Soldaten* (1958–64), Nono's political stage works – *Intolleranza 1960, Al gran sole carico d'amore* (1972–75/78) – or Joan Littlewood's semi-musical *Oh What a Lovely War* (1963), in fact, the work under discussion is a production of Alfons Paquet's (1881–1944) *Fahnen* (*Flags*) from 1924, and the author is the theatre director Erwin Piscator, originator of the so-called documentary play; yet the parallels with what has since become known as hauntology in the arts are quite remarkable. The influential director and actor Gordon Craig (1872–1966), whose radical approaches to dramaturgy drove many innovations in twentieth-century theatre-making, especially in what would become the field of theatre as social practice, was similarly inspired by technology, stating: 'I believe in the time when we shall be able to create works of art in the theatre without the use of the written play, without the use of actors' (Innes, 1972, p.67). Similarities to Craig's vision of inclusive theatre with technology can be observed in Vsevolod Meyerhold's (1874–1940) revolutionary spectacles, whose re-enactments of key events from the Russian Revolution often involved entire towns as 'sets' and huge numbers of the general population as 'actors'.[21] Cage too, experimented with audience participation: both *33⅓* (1969) and *Address* (1977) require the audience to act as 'performers' by operating machinery, while his 'circus' pieces[22] – *Musicircus* (1967), *A House Full of Music* (1981–82) and *Musicircus for Children* (1984) – can accommodate very large numbers of participants (*A House Full of Music* had 800 children playing at its premiere) in shared and inclusive experiences of music performance. Twenty-first-century music-making has taken the concept of the 'non-actor' even further, with digitally conveyed avatars standing in for living performers – the *Abba Voyage* show (2022–ongoing) uses a mixture of recorded vocals and digitally created holograms with a live onstage band – a multimedia approach that Craig and Piscator could only have dreamed of.

---

[21] Pier Paolo Pasolini's (1922–75) work with improvisation and amateur actors and Cornelius Cardew's (1936–81) anti-hierarchical methods share similar traits.

[22] Cage writes: 'By "circus" I mean many pieces going on at once, rather than one alone ... since about '68, ... I have used this principle that I call "musicircus" – of having many things going on at once' (Kostelanetz, 1988, p.84).

Piscator had found contemporary playwriting outmoded and struggled to find quality writing that dealt with political subjects, especially those that showcased Marxist ideology.[23] His work was groundbreaking both in its experimental approach to the technicalities of theatre production and in its consideration of the social function of theatre, traits that will resurface in Nono's work. Like Piscator, Cage also often juxtaposed his technology with a traditional framework. This would not be totally unexpected in a concert setting, but in an operatic one, such as *Europera 5* (1991) – where a Victrola record player, a silent television and a tape machine are all visible onstage – it is far less the norm, drawing parallels between the internal and external spaces of the theatre, as the imaginary and 'real' collide in a melange of modernity. Hauntologically, Cage explicitly confronts the weight of the European operatic canon, combining live performances of arias with tape, historical opera recordings – played on a vintage turntable – radio and TV. Thus, multimedia use brings past and present, near and far, ghosts and the living into collision, questioning the future through technology, but allowing the past to speak through the same means. Cage's choice of a Victrola playing shellac 78s underlines this point. By the 1990s, Victrolas were not particularly common, presenting difficulties in acquisition for performances, and one can imagine the average opera house puzzling over such a tech rider. Perhaps, it was another instance of Cage's desire to showcase virtually obsolete technology – as with the test-tone records of *Imaginary Landscape No. 1* fifty years earlier – to emphasise the temporal gulf between media and performance styles and implicit societal changes.

Piscator employed technology to 'bring the street into the theatre and to link drama with the momentary and real events of the newspaper-world' (Innes, 1972, p.72). As with Nono's overtly expressed political aims, and Cage's experiential sound world, historical legacy is backed up with contemporary documentation and transmission, through film, newspapers, speeches and recordings, as exemplified by Piscator's production of Luise Mühlbach's (1814–73) *The Merchant of Berlin*, whose use of film was at the pinnacle of innovation for the time. In Piscator's words, 'The newspaper is the chronicle of the present instant . . . marks numbered in billions, flicker like a blizzard over the "fourth wall" . . . the antique chorus-form of "mass man" comes photographically, scientifically, objectively to life in this ghost-film of air and newspaper-clippings' (Innes, 1972, p.72). Piscator advocated a comprehensive multimedia approach to technology in performance, 'spreading the load

---

[23] Nono circumvented this problem in the 'azione scenica' *Al gran sole carico d'amore* by constructing the libretto from the speeches and writings of selected political authors, including Karl Marx, Vladimir Lenin, Che Guevara, Fidel Castro and Bertolt Brecht.

of factual data over all the channels of communication, visual and aural' (Innes, 1972, p.77). Projections, films, placards, speeches, photographs and loudspeakers could be observed in his work in an attempt to present objective and factual accuracy simultaneously, while also reflecting the position of technology in everyday life for an audience living in a highly mechanised and industrialised time. The inclusion of contemporary scientific developments in media and communication allowed him to embed politics, history and social commentary into the illusory medium of the stage. Thus, the projection screen – a theatrical tool also used extensively by Joan Littlewood in *Oh What a Lovely War* nearly forty years later[24] – was used to present factual information as a counterpoint to the live stage action.[25] Piscator realised that film could be used to present sweeping yet disparate historical overviews, drawing parallels between different periods and between political and economic subject matter, thereby establishing relevance with the action on the stage. Cage also considered advances in technology as being vital to the continuation of his creative process, keeping abreast of developments in audio recording and dissemination such as radio, optical sound on film, turntables, records, tape and computers.

Piscator viewed his materials, including technology, as the starting points for an eventual dramaturgy, with form deriving from content – and thus open to constant variability – depending on the documentation available for each performance, supported by his extensive reliance on collaboration and improvisation. Last-minute alterations were common and, as Innes (1972, p.80) notes, 'the final version of a play could only be created in rehearsal'. There are some resonances here with both Cage's and Nono's working practices. Nono's approach to composition, trialling multiple fragments with his performers, is reminiscent of Piscator's performer- and material-driven approach, while the vast majority of works involving recorded media will by necessity have a fragmentary approach either during their composition – field/recording, splicing/editing, over-recording/dubbing – or performance or both, while also seeking to emphasise the inherent tensions between recording and live performance. For both Cage and Nono, technological content was a principal component, often driving form, even if only in the sense of a timed 'scaffold' in which to collage multiple sound sources.

---

[24] Littlewood commented, 'only by using "the most recent scientific and technical developments can we create a theatrical form sufficiently flexible to reflect the rapidly changing twentieth-century scene"' (Innes, 1972, p.82).

[25] After a West End performance, Jackie Fletcher recalled that 'The slide projections depicting the reality of trench warfare ... juxtaposed to scenes in which upper class twits ... flounder in incompetence ... finally made sense of a war which sacrificed the working-classes of all nationalities for the benefit of the status quo' (Leach, 2006, p.162).

3 Cage and the Phonograph

... a round steel globe, out of the side of which sprang a gramophone trumpet of curious construction.

– E. F. Benson, 'And the Dead Spake –'[26]

3.1 Recording as Hauntological Curation

As a temporal, ephemeral and frequently social practice, live music-making differs from the carefully curated approach adopted by most modern recordings. Contingency, 'accident' and greater or lesser ratios of performer agency throw the unpredictability of chance into the live experience; as Heaton comments, 'wrong notes, untidy ensemble or imperfect intonation in live performance are, to some extent, the fragile nature of the business' (Heaton, 2009, p.217), but performers and listeners should always be mindful 'that a recording and a performance are two entirely different endeavours' (Heaton, 2009). That the recording as object is inherently hauntological can be observed through its possibilities for spatio-temporal decentring, its ghostly ontology and its affinities with the 'medium of the media', but further hauntological layers are present within the process of recording itself. As Derrida observed in *Cinders* (2014, pp.7–8)[27]:

> What is involved in this phonographic act? Here's an interpretation, one among others. At each syllable, even at each silence, a decision is imposed: it was not always deliberate or sometimes even the same from one repetition to the other. And what it signs is neither the law nor the truth. Other interpretations remain possible – and doubtless necessary. Thus we analyze the resource this double text affords us today: on the one hand, a graphic space opened to multiple readings, in the traditional form of the book ... but on the other hand, simultaneously, and also for the first time, we have the tape recording of a singular interpretation, made one day ... calculated and by chance.

Thus, it is a double text – the score (or 'book') and the recording, complete and yet comprising multiple decisions, voluntary and involuntary, during the recording process. Added to this 'live' recording activity is the curation, or process, towards that final 'singular interpretation', comprising myriad recorded and archived ghostly revenants remaining as virtual fragments. This ghostly ontology is exponentially increased when multi-tracking is added to the

---

[26] Benson, 2012, p.206.
[27] In response to Antoinette Fouque's request to record a version of the text for inclusion in her Éditions des femmes, the 1987 French edition of *Cinders* was accompanied by a cassette recording of the text. Made by Derrida and Carole Bouquet, this recording also featured recorded excerpts of Karlheinz Stockhausen's *Stimmung* for six voices (1968) (Wolfe, 2014, p.viii).

mix, allowing performers to record simultaneously in different locations, or to duet with their own ghostly doubles, and even more so when a record is incorporated into another performance, or the record(s) are the performance, as in *33⅓*. And let us not forget that the phonograph's means of recording, whether cylinder or disc, revolves. It is a revenant itself, with an inbuilt cyclical ontology. The recording forces the live performance (which itself was a 'fixed' moment drawn from an endless lexicon of performative possibilities) into a format where it can be replayed until it breaks and is no longer audible. The immediacy and sociability of the original live event is gone, but as Christian Marclay (2014, p.25) says, 'records are about dead sounds, but when I bring records into a performance and play with them, I change my role from a passive listener to an active player; the same is true for the audience. I give a new life to these dead sounds'. Whether or not listening is a passive activity is subjective, the social and performance possibilities for the audio-document – its 'afterlife' – open up many avenues.

3.2 Cage and Records

In his first collection of writings, *Silence*, John Cage advocated for a new approach to composition and, by extension, performance and reception. This new approach was to have been enabled by the application of technology to all aspects of music-making, and Cage already mentions most of the technologies that would come to hold a prominent position in his music practice. Cage (1961a, p.6) requested that:

> centers of experimental music must be established. In these centers, the new materials, oscillators, turntables, generators, means for amplifying small sounds, film, phonographs, etc., available for use. Composers at work using twentieth-century means for making music. Performances of results. Organization of sound for extra-music purposes (theatre, dance, radio, film).

During conversations with Joan Retallack in 1991, although the subject of discussion was ostensibly Cage's approach to the visual arts, he drew parallels with earlier manual tape splicing techniques and that technology's continuing appeal to him as a creative artist: 'I'm still attracted, even at this point in technology, . . . to the idea of cutting things up and putting them together. . . . One of the troubles with some technology is that it makes it almost impossible to use collage. It makes it so easy to produce an effect with a blurring-over' (Retallack, 1996, p.94). This wariness of the ease of technological 'quick-fixes' may go some way to explaining his prolonged use of 'old-school' analogue technologies, such as records, radio and cassette tapes, despite the ubiquity of the compact disc by the 1990s. As he happily embraced evolving computer technology until his death, there was an evident appeal to the challenges and sound-world inherent in analogue equipment, where the medium itself is prominent, and its sonic and hauntological identity is foregrounded through audible static, hiss, pops and crackles and obvious stops, starts and changes of record, cassette or radio station. Encompassing records, tape, radio, television, film and computers either in performance or to facilitate aspects of his compositional practice, or both, Cage's use of technology was experimental and innovative, yet also backward-looking, embracing ghosts from the past as well as ghosts of the future.

From the 1930s, Cage extolled the importance of technology – turntable included – in music. In 'The Future of Music: Credo' he states: 'Given four film phonographs, we can compose and perform a quartet for explosive motor, wind, heartbeat, and landslide. TO MAKE MUSIC . . . WILL CONTINUE AND INCREASE UNTIL WE REACH A MUSIC PRODUCED THROUGH THE AID OF ELECTRICAL INSTRUMENTS . . . WHICH WILL MAKE AVAILABLE FOR MUSICAL PURPOSES ANY AND ALL SOUNDS THAT CAN BE HEARD' (Cage, 1961a, pp.3–4 [emphasis in original]). Cage was insistent that such technologies should not in any way merely replicate existing acoustic instruments, or that their means and style of performance should be rooted in the past; rather, the variability and opportunities for control of a new, technologically generated sound world would revolutionise the production of sound for music-making, taking advantage of 'PHOTOELECTRIC, FILM, AND MECHANICAL MEDIUMS FOR THE SYNTHETIC PRODUCTION OF MUSIC' (Cage, 1961a, p.4 [emphasis in original]).

Cage's experimental approaches to recording media and technologies can be divided into six subsets:

1. Instrument – where the turntable, radio set, tape player or television are used to either insert sonic found objects into a pre-existing acoustic structure, such as in *Credo in Us* (1942), or where technologically enabled sound content forms the basis for or totality of the work, such as *Radio Music* (1956) and *33⅓* (1969). Another approach involved the audience as performers, as can be seen in *33⅓* and *Address* (1977). Use of the word 'player' with both 'record' and 'cassette' gives a *pharmakon*-like play on words, for who is playing here, the machines or the humans or both? This is amply demonstrated in *Improvisation IV* (1980/82), where Cage asks for 'three cassette players' – both machine and human are 'players', with machine-as-performer built into the name.[28]

---

[28] Cage's ambivalence towards making recordings – rather than *records* as objects – is well documented; for example, to Wilfred Mellers in 1965 he wrote, 'I have as you know very little interest in recordings' (Kuhn, 2016, p.308).

2. Process – where inherent qualities present in processes of playing and/or recording technologies are exploited for musical means, such as in *Cartridge Music* (1960), while *Lecture on the Weather* (1975) involves live tape-mixing during performance.
3. Deconstructed technology – where part of a machine is used for musical means, such as a record player arm or cartridge (needle head), as in *Imaginary Landscape No. 2 (March No. 1)* (1942) and *Cartridge Music*.
4. Means or place of dissemination, or recording as performance – where a performance or recording space is a required part of the performance. *Imaginary Landscape No. 1* (1939) was intended to take place within a radio recording studio and to be performed as a recording or broadcast, while *27' 10.554" for a Percussionist* (1956) can be performed as a recording. Cage's *Water Walk* (1959) is scored for a 'solo television performer' (Cage, 1961c, title page). Cage composed radio plays in the style of classic *Hörspielen*, including *Fifteen Domestic Minutes* (1982) and *Empty Mind* (1987), and other more traditional approaches to radio, such as his *Music for 'The City Wears a Slouch Hat'* (1942). He was a regular broadcaster on TV and radio, often in dialogue with other composers. *Radio Happenings* (1966–67), a series of four conversations with Morton Feldman recorded in New York and broadcast by WBAI, is one such example (Cage & Feldman, 1993).
5. Technological 'extras' – *Imaginary Landscape No. 1* utilises Victor Frequency Records (test-tone records) sliding between 10,000 and 30 Hz (Cage, 1960b).
6. Compositional aids – Cage used computers extensively, most frequently for generating *I Ching* numbers. *HPSCHD* (1967–69), in collaboration with Lejaren Hiller, utilised the ILLIAC II computer mainframe at the University of Illinois, while Cage's only sound and light installation, *Voiceless Essay* (1986–87), incorporated a computer-generated tape.

Cage's first composition involving records, and one of the earliest examples of electronic music, was *Imaginary Landscape no. 1* (1939) for four players. The piece, composed while Cage was at the Cornish School in Seattle, took advantage of the institution's on-site recording and broadcasting equipment and facilities. The performance was housed in two studios, with sounds picked up by individual microphones and mixed separately in the control booth (Kuhn, 2019, p.8). The orchestra, as Cage called it, consisted of a large Chinese cymbal, string piano, and test-tone records of constant frequency (Victor Constant Note Record No. 24 (84519 B)) and variable frequency (Victor Frequency Record 84522 A and Victor Frequency Record 84522 B). All three records were to be played on variable-speed turntables, at 33⅓ or 78 rpm, operating a clutch mechanism on the turntable to produce the effect of pitch sliding, while rhythm was articulated by lifting and lowering the needle head. In conversation with Thom Holmes, Cage remarked: 'We had clutches on those machines that allowed us to produce slides. You didn't shift from 33⅓ to 45 rpm, for instance, but you could go gradually through the whole thing' (Holmes, 2020, p.274). Cage does not seem to have intended this work necessarily to be performed live. This was implied in a 1959 letter to Peter Yates, where Cage simply refers to *Imaginary Landscape I* as 'on Town Hall record',[29] but Yates reinforced this position the following year in a review for *Arts and Architecture*, where he notes: 'The first of several *Imaginary Landscapes* anticipates *musique concrete* [*sic*]. It is a composed recording, using telephone company testing records'[30] and 'Cage's intention in *Landscape No. 1* was to compose a work which would be as a recording the equivalent of an easel painting' (quoted in Iddon, 2020, p.116). Cage was fully aware of the problems of technological obsolescence; the concept of *Landscape No. 1* as a recording takes this difficulty into account, Cage noting that 'the turntables that we had then one no longer sees' (Kostelanetz, 1988, p.157).[31] Hauntologically, Cage is operating in a number of complementary ways: using records in performance, and recording and broadcasting the performance for subsequent iterations, while the operation of the clutch mechanisms and needle-head constantly bring the medium itself to the foreground. For twenty-first-century performers, records are themselves symbols of 'lost' futurity, while in many ways *Landscape No. 1* is also prescient of the techniques of contemporary turntablism, as exemplified by artists such as Christian Marclay, whose live disc-cutting and editing techniques can be traced back to an older heritage.

Cage's choice of the word 'imaginary' in the title is an interesting one; conjuring up images of something unreal, or existing only in the mind, Cage's very tangible ensemble seems anything but 'imaginary'. In a 1973 letter to Peter Naumann, Cage explained: 'I have always used the term "Imaginary Landscape" in connection with works involving technology. That is why they were not called Landscapes' (Kuhn, 2016, p.438). Although Cage refers to a different selection of pieces in the letter – *Winter Music, Water Music, Bird Cage* and so on – the point is valid for his series of five *Imaginary Landscapes*, where sounds are captured and mediated before being deployed in a live concert or a simple playback context. The strangeness of the

---

[29] Described by Cage in a letter to Peter Yates of 1959 as: 'First is on Town Hall record. Second, I hope has been lost. It was like the first as far as instrumentation goes but fancy rather than stark. The third is for percussion orchestra and a great deal of machinery, was done at Museum of Modern Art in 1943. The 4th is for 12 radios and is also entitled *March No. 2*. The 5th is on tape and is fragments of 43 jazz records spliced together' (Kuhn, 2016, p.212).

[30] Yates appears to have been mistaken regarding the origin of the records. Those used by Cage were RCA Victor test-tone records.

[31] The issue of obsolescence is a knotty one for contemporary musicians, especially those specialising in HIPEX (historically informed performance of experimental music).

sound world may go some way to explaining the title also. Although Cage's deployment of electronic media in *Imaginary Landscape No. 1* is not that revolutionary, as Pritchett (1996, p.20) notes, it is 'striking . . . for the effective and *imaginative* [my emphasis] musical use of these records' that others would have regarded as 'just a utilitarian test-tone recording'. Cage's innovative piece was by no means the first to incorporate the turntable. Ottorino Respighi (1879–1936) had experimented with a disc recording of nightingale song for a live performance of *The Pines of Rome* (*Pini di Roma*) in 1924, while both Paul Hindemith (1895–1963) and Ernst Toch (1887–1964) had made trials with the record player as an instrument in its own right, exploiting the medium's playback possibilities by altering the speed, and consequently the pitch, of the material.[32]

An important hauntological consideration present in all these works is the foregrounding of the medium itself through the sonic identifier of 'crackle', a dominant consideration in contemporary musical hauntology. Although Cage did not deliberately choose to emphasise the sound of the phonograph disc itself, anyone familiar with vintage recordings will immediately associate those distinctive crackles and pops with the medium. If a disc is scratched or acquires more scratches during performance, then that identity is exponentially increased; the disc accrues a growing archive of damage on its 'skin' on top of the recorded archive that it already holds. Derrida (1996, p.20) comments:

> Again, inscribing inscription, it commemorates in its way, effectively, a circumcision. A very singular monument, it is also the document of an archive. In a reiterated manner, it leaves the trace of an incision *right on* the skin: more than one skin at more than one age. . . . Each layer here seems to gape slightly, as the lips of a wound, permitting glimpses of the abyssal possibility of another depth destined for archaeological excavation.

The scratches become part of the archive, and the record's appearance changes as a fabric-like patination of warp and weft accumulates on its surface. In the same way that writing cuts into the surface of the paper, the action can be sensed through the absence left by the cut. As a spiral cut itself, the incision is a fundamental part of the recording process – thus a damaged record is a double cut and its archive speaks as music, crackle or both. Its sonic 'ghosts' are still, in a way, a 'living' presence, what Derrida (1996, p.62) refers to as phantoms:

> Perhaps he does not respond, but he speaks. A phantom speaks . . . this means that without responding it disposes of a response, a bit like the answering machine whose voice outlives its moment of recording: you call, the other person is dead, now, whether you know it or not, and the voice responds to you . . .

---

[32] See Holmes (2020, p.192) for more information.

3.3 Early Works: 1939–1952

If we compare works by Cage that incorporate records with those that utilise tape (Tables 1 and 2), the newer medium of tape has a much greater place in Cage's output. However, as Cage worked with records consistently in every decade from the 1930s to the 1990s – moving in step with advances in sound design and materials – we can assume he must have had some fondness for the medium, often combining it with other newer technologies too, as in the *Europeras*.[33]

In Cage's second *Imaginary Landscape*,[34] for five percussionists, again the turntable is used instrumentally, but here only a part – the phonograph tonearm (and cartridge) – is required, used as an amplifier for a coil of wire attached to it, which is played by plucking with a fingernail or stroking it with a handkerchief, an effect Cage had observed when working with radio sound effects technicians (Pritchett, 1996, p.20). Referring to *Imaginary Landscape No. 3* (1942), which uses the same technique, Cage later recalled 'I worked with the sound effects engineer at the radio station in Chicago and he showed me the thunderous sound of the coil of wire in a contact microphone – which I loved' (Kostelanetz, 1988, p.158). Reminiscent of his earlier percussion ensembles, especially the *Third Construction* (1941), the instrumentation includes electric buzzers, tin cans, water gongs and conch shells. In the third *Imaginary Landscape*, for six percussionists, Cage combined tin cans and muted gong with an increased number of electronic sounds – oscillators, buzzers, amplified radio aerial (wire) attached to the needle head and a recording of generator whine – an amplified marimbula and, again, variable-speed turntables playing frequency records. These early examples of deconstructing technology for musical means echo the first *Landscape*, as non-musical elements – test-tone records, recordings of generator sound, record player tonearm, oscillators and buzzers – are subverted to musical ends in another truly 'imaginary' and hauntological use of technology. The medium of the media is showcased as Cage foregrounds the sonic identity of records, turntables and other technology.

Credo in Us (1942) presents a markedly different approach to the integration of media technology with acoustic performance. Scored for percussion quartet, who play among other things, tin cans, gong, tom-tom, electric buzzers, piano and phonographs or radios, it is a landmark piece, exhibiting Cage's first insertion of recordings of music by other composers into his own work. The use of phonograph and/or radio, notated through indications of duration and volume, anticipates later media works such as *Imaginary Landscape No. 5*

---

[33] Even though, according to Thom Holmes (2020, p.283), Cage did not own a record player.
[34] Not to be confused with the 'lost' *Imaginary Landscape 2* that Cage mentions in his letter to Peter Yates.

Table 1 Compositions for/with records and/or turntable parts

Records	1930s–1940s	1950s	1960s	1970s	1980s	1990s
Turntable as instrument	*Imaginary Landscape No. 1* (1939)		*WBAI* (1960) *33⅓* (1969)	*Address** (1977)		
Parts/systems	*Imaginary Landscape No. 2 (March No. 1)* (1942)		*Cartridge Music* (1960) *Variations VI*** (1966) *Variations VII*** (1966/72)	*Child of Tree* (1975) *Branches* (1976)		
Turntable + instrument(s), voice(s), other	*Imaginary Landscape No. 1* (1939) *Imaginary Landscape No. 3* (1942) *Credo in Us* (1942)	*Imaginary Landscape No. 5* (1952) 'Untitled Event', Black Mountain College (1952)	*Theatre Piece* (1960) *Musicircus* (1967) *Variations II* (1961) *Variations III* (1963) *Variations IV* (1963)	*Paragraphs of Fresh Air* (1979)	*Fifteen Domestic Minutes* (1982) *Rocks* (1986)	*Europeras 3 & 4* (1990) *Europera 5* (1991)
Optional		*Variations I* (1958)		*Variations VIII**** (1967/78) *Inlets* (1977)	*Sculptures Musicales* (1989)	

* *Address* has prominent roles for records (played by the audience) and tape (played by the 'performers').

** *Variations VI* and *VII* both use radio to pick up signals and programmes that would very likely have included broadcasts of records/tape during the 1960s.

*** *Variations VIII* consists of a poster bearing the legend 'no music no recordings', in a work that celebrates absence rather than presence.

Table 2 Works for/with tape

Tape	1930s–1940s	1950s	1960s	1970s	1980s	1990s
Solo tape (mix or as instrument)		Williams Mix (1952) Fontana Mix (1958)	Music for 'The Marrying Maiden' (1960) Rozart Mix (1965)	Bird Cage (1972) 49 Waltzes for the Five Boroughs (1977) Telephones and Birds (1977) Address (1977) Sounday (1977–78) A Dip in the Lake (1978)	Improvisation III (1980) Improvisation IV (1980/82) Instances of Silence (1982) HMCIEX (1984) Voiceless Essay (1986–87)	Five Hanau Silence (1991)
Tape + instrument(s), voice(s), other	Music for 'The City Wears a Slouch Hat' (1942) Music for 'Works of Calder' (1949–50)	Imaginary Landscape No. 5 (1952) 27' 10.554" for a Percussionist (1956) Music Walk (1958) Sounds of Venice (1959)	WBAI (1960) HPSCHD (1967–69)	Score (40 Drawings by Thoreau) and 23 Parts (1974) Lecture on the Weather (1975) Paragraphs of Fresh Air (1979) Roaratorio, an Irish Circus on Finnegans Wake (1979)	Ryoanji (double bass) (1983–85) Europeras 1 & 2 (1985–87) Etcetera 2/4 Orchestras (1985) Rocks (1986)	The Beatles 1962–1970 (1990) Europera 5 (1991)

Table 2 (cont.)

	1930s–1940s	1950s	1960s	1970s	1980s	1990s
Tape						
Parts/systems			*Variations VI* (1966) *Variations VII** (1966/72)			
Optional		Black Mountain College 'Untitled Event' (1952) *Variations I* (1958)	*Variations II* (1961) *Music for Carillon No. 4* (1961) *Variations III* (1963) *Variations IV* (1963) *Variations V* (1965) *Variations VI** (1966) *Musicircus* (1967)	*Apartment House 1776* (1976) *Variations VIII*** (1976–78) *Inlets* (1977)		

* *Variations VI* and *VII* both use radio to pick up signals and programmes that would very likely have included broadcasts of records/tape during the 1960s.
** *Variations VIII* consists of a poster bearing the legend 'no music no recordings', in a work that celebrates absence rather than presence.

(1952), *Speech 1955* (1955) and *Radio Music* (1956). In the score's preface, Cage suggests the types of music that would be appropriate for each kind of media: if using radio, 'avoid news programs during national or international emergencies', if using phonograph, 'use some classic: e.g. Dvorak, Beethoven, Sibelius or Shostakovich' (Cage, 1962, preface). In a 1982 letter to Larry Duckles, Cage describes *Credo* as 'a suite of satirical character composed within the phraseology of the dance by Merce Cunningham and Jean Erdman for which it was written' (Kuhn, 2016, p.515). This rather bald statement implies a multitude of possibilities, hauntological, historical, political and personal from US involvement in World War II to the beginnings of Cage and Cunningham's personal relationship. The variability inherent in works utilising records and radio could be read as an all-embracing approach to culture, presenting the *Us/US* of *Credo* as an affirmation of humanity's ability to ultimately transcend conflict during the dark days of World War II, or, as with the *Europera* series (1985–91), in a more nuanced approach to the reuse of existing music, both live and recorded. A Sebaldian reading would surely be bleaker in tone than Cage's light-hearted remarks, emphasising the poisoned legacy of eighteenth- and nineteenth-century (and earlier) European expansion, while reflecting on the far greater capacity for destruction and devastation presented by twentieth-century warfare. A haunted legacy indeed, where supposedly long-dead spectres have the power to rupture, unsettle and return to the present in a 'plural manifestation of the many different ways in which our culture and our politics are shaped by the revisions and repetitions of the past' (Coverley, 2020, p.20). The word 'credo' is an interesting choice too, overloaded with a Christian sense of linear temporality, yet placed by Cage in a deeply hauntological setting, where the revenant, more akin to conceptions of pre-Christian cyclical and mythological time, dominates. Was Cage's suggested record choice merely pragmatic, or indicative of wider considerations of nationalism, revolution, freedom, censorship and constraint? Does *Credo* lay some of these hauntological ghosts to rest by chopping canonical works from Western music history into fragments and subsuming them into an exhilarating cacophony of hammered pots and pans, or does the cacophony merely serve to emphasise the indestructible weight of historical legacy?[35]

Created in 1952, the same year as *Williams Mix*, *Imaginary Landscape No. 5* is Cage's first use of magnetic tape, taking the form of an eight-track collage made from pre-recorded and spliced fragments of any forty-two phonograph

---

[35] Although entirely acoustic, *Three Places in New England* (1911–14, 1929) by Charles Ives (1874–54) plays with similar ideas of quotation, collage and mobile sound in its three movements: 'The "St. Gaudens" in Boston Common (Col. Shaw and His Colored Regiment)', 'Putnam's Camp, Redding, Connecticut' and 'The Housatonic at Stockbridge'.

records, and was made in collaboration with David Tudor and electronic film-music pioneers Bebe and Louis Barron. It was originally composed to accompany Jean Erdman's dance solo *Portrait of a Lady*, and Cage's record choice for his realisation was certainly important in this regard, echoing the influence of jazz in Erdman's choreography and that of her dance class (Fetterman, 2010, p.19). However, Cage also felt that using chance procedures to determine content might be a good way to remove issues of personal taste, especially concerning music not particularly to his liking, such as jazz (Fetterman, 2010, p.20).[36] Unlike *Credo in Us*, the score includes no suggestions as to which recordings to use, instead leaving the choice entirely at the 'performer's' – compositor's – discretion. The published score, a Feldman-like block graph, with each square representing three inches of tape, was constructed by Cage using the *I Ching*. Thus, *Imaginary Landscape No. 5* is a chance-constructed framework in which to fit LP content that is performer-driven, and thus indeterminate. This is amply demonstrated by the plethora of versions currently available to listen to, ranging from classical and opera to jazz, pop, environmental sound and electronica, made that much easier by the options for splicing and arrangement now opened up by the DAW. Interestingly, although Cage, Tudor and the Barrons' original was made for tape, Cage notes in the score that 'the record, used in performance, may be tape or disc' (Cage, 1961b, unnumbered instruction page), although this may merely be a pragmatic suggestion for a more readily available medium for playback in early 1952. In some ways, it is quite surprising to find tape pieces that are open to infinite variation. However, even Cage's more substantial tape works, such as *Williams Mix* (1952) and *Fontana Mix* (1958), have the potential to be newly minted, with scores existing for both works that could potentially be realised by others.[37] Cage's approach to variability and non-permanence changes the ways in which we think about recording technologies. Not only are they the media of ghosts, but the ghosts have the potential to change radically with each new visitation. Cage's record (and radio) collages prefigure late 1990s and early noughties hauntological music, not only in their overall sound world – scratchy shellac (or vinyl), missed grooves, sudden dynamic alterations and extreme fragmentation – but also in

---

[36] Cage had similar approaches to overcoming his dislike of environmental radio sounds, mentioning to Morton Feldman in 1966, 'you know how I adjusted to that problem of the radio in the environment ... I simply made a piece using radios. Now, whenever I hear radios ... I think, "Well, they're just playing my piece"' (Cage & Feldman, 1993, pp.11–13).

[37] The 'score' for *Williams Mix* resembles a dressmaker's pattern, indicating the tape manipulation of six subcategories of sounds, utilising tiny fragments made with angled, rather than vertical, cuts. Cage recalled that 'the score has nearly five hundred pages and, therefore, it has not been reproduced ... I have illustrated it in the notes to the Town Hall program' (Kostelanetz, 1988, p.163).

their mode of operation. By scrambling a chance-derived mixture of inexpensive records, especially when these are combined with radio, Cage is laying the groundwork for hauntological artists such as the Caretaker, who will use vintage records fifty years later for a similar aesthetic, but through the interface of the DAW.

Considered to be the first proto-happening, and an important precursor to the field of performance art, is the 'Untitled Event' at Black Mountain College of 1952. Only scraps of what could loosely be termed a score remain, but what does seem to be agreed upon, via performer and audience recollections of the event, is that it was a multimedia, multi-performer collage of independent and sometimes simultaneous but unrelated events. Dance, poetry, theatre,[38] a lecture, records and radio, a piano, film, slides, paintings and a small dog were all present, in a mix that foreshadows Cage's multimedia extravaganza *HPSCHD* in the following decade. Cage noted that the audience was part of the event – 'In each one of the seats was a cup, and it wasn't explained to the audience what to do with this cup . . . but the performance was concluded by a kind of ritual of pouring coffee into each cup' (Kirby & Schechner, 1965, p.52) – prefiguring *33⅓* and *Address*, where audience participation is explicit in the published scores. Phonograph records were played by both David Tudor and Robert Rauschenberg, the latter using an old-fashioned 78 rpm model with a horn. Record choice is uncertain, but Édith Piaf and popular music from the 1920s and 30s are both possibilities (Fetterman, 2010, p.101). Two important trends emerge from the event: the record player as an instrument of (ghostly) disruption – building on Cage's work in the 1940s – and its part in a wider mobile hierarchy of sensory experiences. The addition of records into an already complex event further adds to the sense of disruptive decentring, and Cage's inclusion of fresh coffee means that the auditory, olfactory, visual, somatic and gustatory senses are all engaged. Cage summed up this sense of interpenetration in *Composition in Retrospect*, written nearly three decades later and composed in the form of a mesostic:

> musIcircus / maNy / Things going on / at thE same time / a theatRe of differences together / not a single Plan / just a spacE of time / aNd / as many pEople as are willing / performing in The same place / a laRge / plAce a gymnasium / an archiTecture / that Isn't / invOlved / with makiNg the stage // dIrectly opposite / the audieNce and higher / Thus / morE / impoRtant than where they're sitting / the resPonsibility / of Each / persoN *is* / marcEl duchamp said / To complete / the woRk himself / to heAr / To see / orIginally / we need tO / chaNge. (Cage, 1993, p.24)[39]

---

[38] The poets M. C. Richards and Charles Olsen both climbed a ladder from which to recite poetry (Fetterman, 2010, p.98).
[39] I have highlighted the capitals in bold for ease of reading the spine word INTERPENETRATION.

3.4 Innovation in the 1960s: Cage and the Cartridge

Cage had long been interested in using parts of the turntable, invariably in ways that involved theatre as much as music. Theatricality would become an increasingly important component of Cage's practice from the 1950s onwards, coming to full fruition in the 1960s, a decade in which Cage composed a slew of pieces that are as invested in process and theatre as they are conventional music. These included works involving tape, records, radio, television and electronics, as well as more conventional instrumental means of sound production, with the resulting experience being akin to the sensory overload of the traditional three-ring circus, a comparison made by Peter Yates. In his review of *Cartridge Music* (1960) in 'John Cage's Weekend in Los Angeles' (1962), Yates recalled:

> Do you remember the three rings, the three shows going on at once, the too much of everything that the eye could not take in? . . . Here before us were the three rings, three speakers, that we could not take in, and at the center, before them, solemnly going about their nonsensical or useless business, the two actors, composer and pianist, had become two clowns. . . . It wasn't a joke; it wasn't funny in that sense; it was nonsense, release, hilarious. I don't know when I have laughed so freely. (in Iddon, 2020, pp.197–98)

This comment was triggered after Yates witnessed Cage and Tudor manipulating the prepared cartridges[40] through striking and rubbing, also producing unearthly shrieks and whines, as pieces of furniture were dragged across the floor, all amplified by the cartridges and contact mics, and relayed over a speaker system. The collage of variable sounds and actions, many repurposed from everyday life, recall artistic bricolage, a theme that is also of interest to Derrida as part of wider questions of decentring. Although *bricolage* is perhaps a term most usually associated with the visual arts, where it refers to the assemblage of items taken out of their normative contexts and repurposed for artistic ends, it may also be applied in other contexts. Bricolage encourages the general rather than the specific: within a given culture or heritage, objects, practices, sounds and so on can be combined and freely adapted to other uses, to new uses, even if they thereby contradict their original function or operation. So, bricolage works within and against a heritage: it undermines the system from within, like hauntology, it makes time out of joint by decentring discourse. In *Cartridge Music* Cage continues his odyssey of decentring music – and the turntable, literally – by embracing a plurality of sound and action. It's no coincidence that Cage would also write his *Theatre Piece* (1960), the

---

[40] Cage and Tudor added slinky toys, feathers, sticks, wire, toothpicks, pipe cleaners, nails and screws, tiny flags and cocktail parasols to the cartridges during a performance in 1961 (Fetterman, 2010, p.64).

Variations series (1958–78), *Musicircus* (1967) and the apogee of Cage's 'circus' and multimedia performance pieces, *HPSCHD*, during this decade.

By the time Cage composed *Cartridge Music*, turntable technology had improved enormously from his earlier experiments in the *Imaginary Landscapes* series. In a 1960 letter to David Tudor, Cage writes: 'About the Cartridge Music (unwritten so far). I will bring cartridges with me, but the number we will use will depend on the loudspeakers and amplifiers available. These <u>must</u> be of good or excellent quality. . . . I will bring 1 or 2 dozen cartridges' (Iddon, 2013, p.119). To the twenty-first-century musician, unless they are particularly invested in vinyl, reading a request for a 'cartridge' in one of Cage's score can be somewhat perplexing. The cartridge is actually one of the six fundamental parts of a record player: the cartridge/styli, tonearm and counterweight, platter, record spindle, plinth and motor. Sitting at the end of the tonearm, above the stylus or needle, the cartridge is a crucial component in an analogue sound's journey from record groove to speaker. The cartridge body holds the suspension and the stylus-housing cantilever, the coils (or magnets) that amplify the signal from the stylus and four output pins. Amplitude is dependent on whether the cartridge type is a moving magnet or a moving coil. Thus, when Cage asks for a 'cartridge' he is – to put it very simply – asking for a mini-amplifier or contact microphone, depending on the piece in question. Thus, the wire attached to the tonearm in *Imaginary Landscape No. 1* uses the cartridge principally for amplification, producing the unearthly sounds that so attracted Cage in the radio studio. Although Cage does precisely identify what a cartridge is in the score of *Cartridge Music* – writing, 'A cartridge is an ordinary phonograph pick-up in which customarily a playing needle is inserted', and 'Instead of a playing needle, any object that will fit into a cartridge may be inserted (e.g., a coil of wire, a toothpick, a pipe-cleaner, a twig, etc.)' (Cage, 1960a, instruction sheet) – by the 1970s, the performer was expected to know this, and no further explanation is given in the later scores.[41]

Hauntologically, the cartridge is a loaded device, functioning on two separate levels. It is emblematic of the turntable as a machine, and the ghosts of its scientific and cultural history; it embodies the many different genres that have been played on it, from office dictation to orchestral classics, contemporary jazz to rock 'n' roll, environmental recordings to sound art and the avant-garde. As a fragment of the machine itself, it also resonates with contemporary usage, the 'crate digging' of twenty-first-century hauntology, whose delight in repurposing the revenant – the lost, discarded and forgotten discs of

---

[41] Made doubly confusing for non-US performers, who may know the cartridge simply as the 'needle-head'.

yesteryear – aligns with the cartridge's status as a component, no longer as a fixed part of the turntable but liberated and repurposed by Cage and Tudor as part of the *act* of performance and also as fundamental to creating the performance *score*. The score of *Cartridge Music* is like a kit, consisting of a sheet of instructions, pages with irregular shapes drawn on them and a number of transparencies.[42] The number of cartridges determines which pages of irregular shapes to use, with further details, such as cartridge changes, determined by the transparencies. Thus, everything depends upon that initial choice of cartridge, with resulting sounds being generalised rather than specific. The year 1960 also saw the composition of *Theatre Piece*, one of Cage's most complex uses of indeterminate notation. Generated from the score of *Fontana Mix* (1958), *Theatre Piece* can be realised by one to eight performers for a duration of thirty minutes. The means to initiate sound actions are left to each player's discretion, indicated by a choice of twenty words (nouns or verbs), to be interpreted as actions. David Tudor played phonograph records in the premiere – at New York's Circle in the Square theatre (March 1960) – along with making tea, running around and crawling underneath the piano and playing with assorted items of party ephemera (Fetterman, 2010, p.112). Cage reused the musicircus approach quite regularly during the 1960s, not least in *33⅓*, and also in the works for the US bicentennial in 1976 – *Renga* and *Apartment House 1776*.

3.5 Cage's *33⅓* (1969)

The genesis of *33⅓* began in the autumn semester of 1969 at the University of California, Davis, where Cage was engaged to teach a course for the music department. Student enrolment was impressive at 120, and Cage decided that such a large group would be better served by operating in smaller groups, each using the *I Ching* to both demystify the inner workings of the university library and create a diverse array of *I Ching*-derived outputs (recipes, compositions, films, poems and letters) from this exercise. Cage also decided that he would be more effective if he took on the role of student, rather than teacher, joining different groups as the semester progressed. By a process of *I Ching*-determined reduction, from an area of the library to a single title, Cage hoped that 'one is less likely to be processed by the library's efficiency in categorizing itself; *it*, on the other hand, is being processed by your efficiency in evading its categorical self-analysis' (Dinwiddie, 2011, p.236). This idea resonates strongly with

---

[42] The four transparencies consist of points, circles, a stopwatch motif and a dotted line. These are used to determine time-bracket durations for each action, manner of sound production (for cartridge or auxiliary sounds) and sound quality (including amplitude and tone control) (Cage, 1960a, instruction sheet).

deconstructive approaches to the institution and its archives espoused by Derrida and John D. Caputo. Contained within a broader discussion of Derrida and the academy, Caputo (1987, p.235) comments:

> Institutions are the way things get done, *and* they are prone to violence. They are inextricably, undecidably, pharmacologically both things at once. Nothing is innocent. . . . One needs to operate within the university . . . in order to expose it to its other, to the abyss, to keep its standards and its preconceived notions of rationality in play, to keep reason in play and to keep the play in reason.

Not only did Cage's course aim to bring the library – usually an institution's largest structure – down to the individual human level, but also his methods were subversive in their radical use of chance procedures to disrupt a very non-chance organised body, replete with myriad text 'ghosts'. In practice, the choice of materials led to some extreme results – as well as some extremely prosaic ones – with Dinwiddie noting the concern of one student who had created a chance-derived recipe that demanded prodigious quantities of chilli powder (Dinwiddie, 2011, p.236). Cage's procedures, even though somewhat erratically organised in practice, embodied very effective strategies of decentring within a highly structured milieu – namely, the university.

Utilising 300 LPs and twelve phonographs and to be performed by the audience (Figure 1), the world premiere of *33⅓*, given at the University of California, Davis's music department on 21 November 1969, must have been quite an occasion. The premiere took place during an all-day music event – running from 5:40 a.m. to 12:40 a.m. – devised by Cage called *Mewantemooseicday*[43] that included film screenings, readings, lectures and music performances, including selections of Satie's *Musique d'ameublement* (Furniture music) and 840 repetitions of his *Vexations*, each preceded by a fixed period of meditation and played by a rotating team of pianists. All the events were free to attend, and the audience was encouraged to come and go at will, making the event experience more like visiting an exhibition than a standard Western concert. During Cage's lecture readings, other sounds – equipment testing, sound checks and so on – were deliberately allowed to penetrate into Cage's recitation, echoing his already firmly established use of ambient sound. The performance area allotted to *33⅓* was reached through a continuous orchestral concert of *Musique d'ameublement* taking place simultaneously in the lobby, eventually reaching a hall containing LPs and players ranged around the room, but no seating, as Cage had hoped for free audience-player circulation. The overall effect was 'most of the time,

---

[43] Cage had originally hoped to call the event *Godamusicday*, but was overruled by the university (Dinwiddie, 2011, p.236).

Figure 1 Cage's *33⅓*, Oxford, 2024 performance.

a complex collage of music; however, at one point . . . an older gentleman proceeded to turn everything off, only to have them turned on again almost immediately by other, more gregarious audience/participants' (Dinwiddie, 2011, p.237). The LPs available were chosen by chance, the selection process having been given to the manager of a local record store in Sacramento by Cage, probably resulting in a grand shelf-clearing exercise of difficult-to-sell items. After the performance, most of the LPs disappeared – taken as mementoes by the audience. Throughout the day, several events included the consumption of food as part of the activities, thereby making the audience experience multi-sensory, reminiscent of the coffee-drinking concept originally enacted at Cage's 1952 'Untitled Event' at Black Mountain College. Although composed for records, *33⅓* has remarkable similarities to the practice of the 'mix tape' in the 1970s. In effect, every participant gets to be their own DJ, in an emancipatory exercise in live curation.

From the beginning, *33⅓* is a collective 'circus' experience, where collaboration between participants and 'composer' and tension between the 'live' and the recorded coalesce in one great musical-cultural sonic collage. By giving the initial choice of records to the store owner in Sacramento, and then by further expanding this process during the performance, the premiere of *33⅓* echoes Cage's course and its decentring of the university library. Chance plays a very important role in performance, with the audience having complete agency over the choice of recordings (from within the set of variables provided), the choice of which machine to place a record on and what speed to play it at, the volume, whether to change a record, where to sit or stand and when and where to move. The experience is truly immersive and mobile: not only do individual record choices affect the evolving musical collage, but also those bodies moving in space have a very real effect on the sound spatialisation by opening – or blocking – sonic pathways, depending on their movements. Hence, the 'tele' of 'tele-technology' is represented not only in the obvious form of the record but also for each member of that mobile audience. Sound will travel (bleed) from outside, from within the hall – including the natural conversation that ensues in the performance of such a piece – and between the twelve turntables.[44] The 'tele' and the 'medium of the media' are central concerns, questioning notions of authorship, materiality and what it is to 'perform' within complex and mobile hierarchies.

Although Cage seldom referred to *33⅓*, the few reports that do exist provide extremely useful documentary information for contemporary players. As the

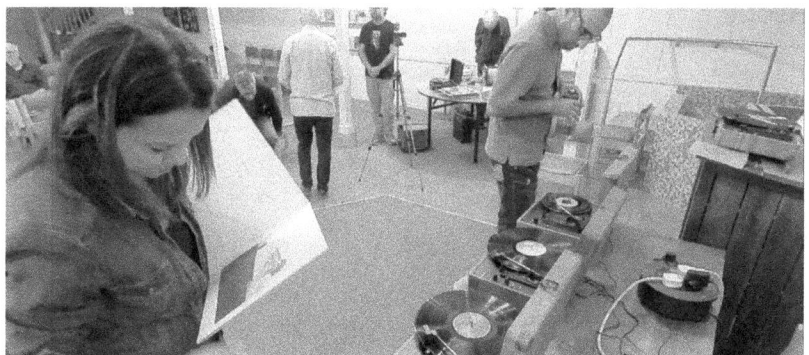

Video 1 John Cage, 33⅓ (1969), New Road Baptist Church, Oxford, UK. August 29th 2024. Video file available at www.Cambridge.org/Lesser

---

[44] The version that was filmed for this volume (Video 1) used eleven turntables, including one vintage machine, and one compact disc player, and had a choice of approximately 350 LPs, 50 45s and 50 CDs. As the original score calls for 8–12 turntables, the inclusion of one CD player was deemed an acceptable compromise.

information written or spoken by Cage on this piece is rather limited, I shall include three of these sources, beginning with the score. The score, which is only an a posteriori description of events, lists the composition's forces and duration, followed by a short description of the premiere:

> In 1969 at the University of California, Davis, I arranged an event called 33 ⅓ which consisted of an auditorium with eight sound systems, the sound sources being recordings played on playbacks. Each playback had a technical assistant who did not himself play the records but who was available in case a member of the 'audience' had difficulty in doing so. For the 'audience' was the performers. Without them nothing was heard. (Cage, 2011, instruction page)

Cage refers to *33⅓* again in a letter from 1977 to the US musicologist Wiley H. Hitchcock:

> Some years ago at Davis in California (1969), I presented a piece called 33⅓. The lobby was filled with musicians (live) playing Satie's *Musique d'A* (3 of the pieces). When a person entered the hall, he saw it was empty except for 12 playbacks, stacks of LP's, 12 lg. speakers, 12 assistants standing at the playback stations and whatever other members of the audience there were already assembled. The fact that he cd. play and/or stop a record finally dawned on each person + if he had trouble with the machine, the asst. would help. (Kuhn, 2016, p.464)

Thirteen years later, during an interview with William Fetterman in 1990, Cage recalled:

> 33–1/3 – That's where the people play the records. When you came into the Hall there were piles of records [300] in front of record players – I think there were twelve – and they were 33–1/3 [r.p.m.]. And there's no one playing them, so that the audience is obligated, if they want any sound, to play them. I just got a large number of records, so that there'd be piles of records in front of each play-back. If they couldn't do it, there were assistants to help them.
>
> It was done first at the University of California at Davis, in a thing called *Mewantemooseicday*. 'Me-Wantem' is a reference to Thoreau, because he asked his Indian guide what he wanted for breakfast, and his answer was 'Me wantem fat' (laughs). So this was *Mewantemooseicday* (laughs) because it was a day full of music. 33–1/3 was in the evening. (Fetterman, 2010, p.142)[45]

---

[45] Dinwiddie (2011, p.236) recalls a slightly different version of this story, noting that, according to Cage, the title originated from Thoreau's journey into the Maine woods, but that 'He asked an old Indian if he knew someone who could help. The Indian replied, "Me will ... *Me wantum moose*."'

Cage's comments provide ample information for performance, and readily available technology makes staging *33⅓* fairly straightforward today. No longer are additional speakers, wiring and cumbersome systems required; instead, portable record players with built-in speakers – echoing the vintage Dansette brand and similar machines from the 1950s and later – make for a considerably more compact set-up. Hauntologically, although vinyl is now much more popular than it was thirty years ago, obtaining 300 LPs is still a relatively demanding requirement, necessitating recourse to charity shops, garage sales, and rifling through boxes of inherited LPs. Thus, each culturally and historically situated realisation of *33⅓* is replete with ghostly revenants, perhaps damaged, mouldy, or missing their covers and sleeves – from the detritus of earlier eras to carefully preserved collector's items, all have come 'back' into use. Many of them bear signs of water damage, small scratches and scuffs, and all are engraved onto a circular, repeating format.[46] By placing twelve record players in a roughly circular design, Cage is imitating the clock face,[47] again suggesting circular time, repetition, ghosts that return, and perhaps, also something a little more sinister. A certain sense of political indoctrination, of justice denied, or even the sonic bombardment of noise torture can be read in such a floor plan, and sonically this three-ring circus is no longer quite so innocent.

As Grubbs (2014, p.76) notes, it's a perfect example of Cage as 'a pioneer in the counterintuitive use of recording technology within *live* performance' (my emphasis). Not only was this performance replete with a great many recorded 'ghosts', but during the performance, the 'ghostliness' of the medium itself would have become more apparent – in an audible demonstration of the passing of time – as needles bouncing on missed grooves and LPs carelessly placed on unfamiliar phonographs acquired a patination of new scratches affecting the sonic experience. Unlike *Imaginary Landscape No. 5*, where found objects are carefully curated and recorded in the studio, in *33⅓* sonic decay is built into the performance itself, balancing nicely with Satie's direction that 'furniture music should do two things: (1) occupy space and (2) *age*' (Dinwiddie, 2011, p.235, my emphasis). Thinking

---

[46] All hauntological analogue recording media are based on circular forms: records (and cylinders) are circular, a record's sound is engraved onto a circular, repeating groove; tape, both cassette and reel to reel, again works on a circular repeating system, as does the compact disc. Radio may appear to be an outlier, but as a broadcaster of tapes and records, it also partakes in this circularity, not least in the repetition of programmes and other catch-up and on-demand services currently available.

[47] In an echo of the conductor's clocklike arm movements in *Theatre Piece* (see Fetterman, 2010, pp.108, 112–13), the four clock-face motifs found on the transparency from *Cartridge Music* and more universal conceptions concerning the temporal, as can be observed in *Atlas Eclipticalis* (1961).

back to Derrida's techno-tele-iconicity and techno-tele-discursivity, *33⅓* fulfils both these basic hauntological tenets. The 'tele' permeates the entire work, with its recorded media embodying 'tele' in space and time, and its mobile audience experiencing a constantly shifting, and consequently 'tele', aural field; but what of discursivity and iconicity? Despite the record's inability to answer back, the documentation of spoken words and music still allows the audience to immerse themselves in a conversation, albeit one-sided, rather in the manner of an answerphone or dictation machine. The voices of the 'dead' are still speaking, and even if spectral, they participate in the discourse, only the audience is now composed of eavesdroppers, occupied in activities closer to surveillance than conversation. 'Iconicity' resonates strongly with broader Marxist themes: the monetary value of goods, the commodification of music and playback systems and the surplus labour paradigm of mass production balanced against the need of 'crate diggers' and 'completists' to possess increasingly obscure versions of recordings and equipment, inflating costs as demand outstrips an ever-dwindling supply, occupying an orbit of 'that which in general assures and determines the *spacing* of public space, the very possibility of the *res publica* and the phenomenality of the political' (Derrida, 2006, p.63). Hence, media as state apparatus of control, as communication without contact, media as both conduit and guardian of information, media to educate and/or indoctrinate and media as palpable manifestation of the public sphere. As such, Cage's semi-happening is the embodiment of late capitalist society; a 'happening' that is spontaneous up to a certain point only, utilising, in the case of the premiere, newly purchased machines and materials, reselling the past as a nod to the future, where 'music' is imprisoned in a vinyl cage, while it is the surrounding environment and audience that supplies the variables of live 'performance'. In *33⅓*, time is indeed 'out of joint', the 'no longer' of the recordings juxtaposed with the 'not yet' of the yearned for utopian society of the future, where authorship is uncertain and traditional hierarchies are fractured and decentred. To record, to archive, is the promise *of* the future, *to* the future. The promise of the archive, as Derrida (1996, p.18) commented in *Archive Fever*, 'as wager [*gageure*]. The archive has always been a *pledge*, and like every pledge [*gage*], a token of the future'. The record, as one of music's ultimate archives, resonates perfectly with Derrida's observation. Cage used recorded materials placed in the context of a live environment, and Nono incorporated acoustic material from a live environment, placed in tension with a live performer (singer), so although there are some apparent oppositions in working practices (live sound/dead sound, performer/audience) it is interesting to note that, fundamentally, both are seeking knowledge of a situation through sound, via practices of active listening.

3.6 Later Works

Cage never gave up on the record, with some of his most interesting, innovative and provocative multimedia works appearing during the 1970s to '90s. In his last works incorporating records, the *Europeras*, Cage was very much anticipating the 'historic recording' revival – in academic and performance research – of the late '90s, as well as the 'recycle, reuse' mantra of the twenty-first-century climate emergency. Expanding ideas already trialled in *33⅓* by adding tape to the hauntological mix, *Address* (1977) saw Cage combine two separate compositions: a performance of *33⅓*, with the audience playing discs on twelve turntables as in the earlier work, and one of *Cassette*, with five 'performers' playing an electric bell as though panellists on a TV show and cassette tapes of Cage's lectures. For good measure, the world premiere also featured simultaneous performances of Satie's music in the ultimate Cagean live 'mix tape'. The year 1977 was auspicious for the record, which received global attention when a 'golden record' of cultural and scientific earth data – including a substantial quantity of music – was launched into space as part of NASA's Voyager probe. Emblematic of time that is 'out of joint', the medium of the media, the 'tele' in all its forms, the temporal implications of space travel, and the lost future of the – now somewhat tarnished – golden age of space exploration, not to mention the ultimate 'mix', it would be difficult to find a more exemplary hauntological object.

Further multimedia compositions by Cage followed *Address*, including *Fifteen Domestic Minutes* (1982) and the *Europeras*. A perfect example of hauntology in action, *Fifteen Domestic Minutes*, for speakers[48] and records, increases the decentring of Cage's classic radio plays but raises the stakes by playing the selected records on several different radio stations simultaneously. *Rocks* (1986) plays with sound spatialisation, delivered by a variable ensemble across combinations of three to five players and sound sources chosen from a selection of radios, televisions, records, microphones and ad-lib cassettes. Here, the sound *sources* are fixed, but by placing them around the performance space and varying the performers working at any one time, the sound moves around the room as though spatialised through a speaker array. Overlaps between groups are discouraged, presumably so that each sonic collective feels doubly centred: historically as a medium and temporospatially, coming from any*where* and any*when*. Explicitly juxtaposing contemporary and vintage technologies in ways that highlight the overturning of traditional narrative concepts of time and space, the last two of the *Europeras* series explicitly

---

[48] The male and female speaker each reads from the first and last six pages of James Joyce's *Finnegans Wake*.

demonstrate Cage's canny use of technology to problematise form, genre, heritage and legacy. Cage had already established a live 'mix' approach to opera in *Europeras 1 & 2* (1987), using chance procedures to determine the unfolding and interpenetration of selected operatic overtures, arias and plots in an overt disruption of one of Western music's most revered and still popular art forms. Cage makes this disruption evident through different means in each of the *Europeras*, using live orchestra, costumes, sets and props in *1 & 2*; a completely stripped stage, disc recordings and no costumes in *3 & 4* (1990) and a multimedia approach in *5* (1991). Cage explained: 'instead of having an orchestra in *3 & 4*, or costumes, or sets, we have just record players which give the sound of the orchestra, but you get many orchestras at once, so that the obstruction increases' (Retallack, 1996, p.226). In other words, by playing many recordings simultaneously, exactly as in *33⅓*, any sense of musical, historical or story narrative is obliterated. All sound, whether historical or contemporary, becomes a wildly curated 'now', caught in a vortex of time that is completely out of joint. In the last *Europera* this disruption is both more historically clear cut through its use of technology and more nuanced, with facets of present and past placed in juxtaposition:

> in *5* the material changes to include radio and television. So that what happens in *5* is a juxtaposition of the two centuries, nineteenth and twentieth. . . . There's no pretense of a twentieth-century opera. Opera is stated as being of the nineteenth century, through the victrola, of which there's only one. . . . Whereas in *3 & 4* there are something like six record players, and each has a stack of fifty to a hundred records, organized through chance. . . . It's quite a marvelous sound because the sound of those old machines has another quality of its own. (Retallack, 1996, p.226)

Not only are the two opposing centuries foregrounded, but so are the media from within the twentieth century. The Victrola indicates a technological past, while TV and radio represent the present. And yet, radio has existed in the popular consciousness for almost as long as the phonograph, while TV is already an outdated medium, its traditional content being accessed as often via phones and computers in the twenty-first century, and streamed instead of live or scheduled. Appropriately enough in one of his last works, Cage returns to the concept of silence: 'a new idea creeps in in *5* which is the opposition of the centuries; and the radio and the television represent the twentieth, obviously, and the television does it silently. Never opens its mouth. Yet it has, so to speak, the last word in the whole piece. So that you're faced with the silence of the twentieth century' (Retallack, 1996, p.226). There are a number of possibilities when it comes to Cage's use of the word 'silence' here. Is he referring to the unrecorded media blanks – records and tapes – whose sonic identities form such a significant part of contemporary hauntology? Seeming visually to revert to the era of silent film, Cage has also dragged the television into the orbit of the Victrola, while simultaneously marking the sensory overload that is the twentieth century, where everything becomes curated data in an eternal hauntological present symbolised by the hum of electrical energy, and where so many voices speak concurrently that the sonic landscape becomes an endless wash of white noise.

4 Nono and Tape

> [KRAPP *switches off impatiently, winds tape forward, switches on again*]
> [KRAPP *switches off, winds tape back, switches on again.*]
> – Samuel Beckett, *Krapp's Last Tape*[49]

Obsessively rewound and fast forwarded, accompanied by repeated cries of Krapp's *idée fixe* 'spool!', ignored, despised and adored throughout the play's duration, the recorded memories of the titular Krapp in Samuel Beckett's *Krapp's Last Tape* (1958) hover somewhere between life and death; they are the ghosts of memories, made from the traces of traces. Even the opening of the play occurs during '*A late evening in the future*' (Beckett, 1990, p.215), as an indication of the central role that time will play in *Krapp*. Yet, like all such recordings, Krapp's constant reworking of the past 'signs . . . neither the law nor the truth' (Derrida, 2014, p.7), for they are merely the recording of a 'moment' and open to multiple interpretations. Krapp's last tape plays on in 'silence' as the curtain closes, the hiss of the medium foregrounded over speech. The word 'spool' is synonymous not only with Beckett's protagonist but also with analogue tape cultures from the late 1940s onwards. As a medium, tape is strongly associated with the immediate post-war dominance of musical modernism, with quasi-totemic figures of the avant-garde, such as Boulez, Stockhausen and Nono – the latter two producing a substantial number of works involving tape – guiding the direction of influential institutions like Darmstadt in a febrile cauldron of political and artistic upheaval.

Since the mid-1950s, Nono had been considering the possibilities for combining recorded sounds – natural and artificial – with live performance, and the spatialisation that a speaker relay would offer him. He produced a significant number of works that utilised magnetic tape during the 1960s and '70s, exploring the options for recording, producing and transforming sound. Despite having made the transition to electronics in the mid-'70s, Nono did not completely abandon tape as a creative medium, with one of his last works, *La lontananza nostalgica utopica futura. Madrigale per più 'caminantes' con*

---

[49] Beckett, 1990, pp.220, 221.

Gidon Kremer (1988), being composed for solo violin and eight tapes. More broadly, during the post-war period, the revolutionary format of tape, and particularly the cassette tape, had expanded music portability and personal choice in ways that could not have been imagined earlier in the twentieth century. As a committed communist, politics and technology formed a natural partnership for Nono, with tape's convenience allowing him to both record from 'real life' – and thus showcase social and economic inequalities – and share his music with this same demographic in situ. His political beliefs brought him into the orbit of like-minded creatives, with some of the most significant, from a hauntological point of view, being his collaborations with the theatre director Erwin Piscator.

4.1 Nono and Tape: The Early 1960s

As can be seen in Table 3, unlike Cage, who worked with a multiplicity of analogue sonic hauntological technologies – records, radio, audio and video tape and television – Nono confined himself to tape alone, with both composers appreciating tape's flexibility as a format. Even in the early 1950s, when Cage was working on *Williams Mix* (1952) and *Fontana Mix* (1958),[50] despite the intricate and slow pace of composition, the medium was still better suited to being used as a pre-planned creative tool than the record or radio, where by necessity, chance played a much greater role. For Nono, tape's portability made it the ideal medium for making field recordings in places of work, and its flexibility was perfect for executing complex editing and mastering processes, allowing for much greater control of the final 'mix', while its superior sound quality and capacity were also welcomed. Recording multiple layers of sound was now possible through bouncing tracks between machines, allowing composers (and sound engineers) to overdub one sound onto another without losing individual clarity. Obviously, these techniques made multitrack recording much simpler, more controllable and of considerably better sound quality than the cumbersome arrangements that Hindemith and Toch had worked with in their early experiments with overdubbing onto phonograph discs, although it should be noted that by the late 1940s the US performer/producer Les Paul had made many improvements using a disc-to-disc recording technique.

Nono's first foray into tape music, his *Omaggio a Emilio Vedova* (1960), was produced on the RAI Studio di Fonologia's four-track machine, whose half-inch tape offered good sound quality. Additionally, overdubbing was possible on three-, four- and eight-track models, thereby substantially increasing creative

---

[50] Coincidentally, Cage's *Fontana Mix* and Nono's first tape work, *Omaggio a Emilio Vedova*, were both created at Milan's RAI Studio di Fonologia.

Table 3 Works for/with tape

Works for tape	1960s	1970s	1980s
Tape solo	*Omaggio a Emilio Vedova* (1960) *Die Ermittlung* (1965) *Ricorda cosa ti hanno fatto in Auschwitz* (1966) *Contrappunto dialettico alla mente* (1968) *Musiche per Manzù* (1969)	*Für Paul Dessau* (1974)	
Tape and solo instrument/voice	*La fabbrica illuminata* (1964)	*. . . . . sofferte onde serene . . .* (1976)	*La lontananza nostalgica utopica futura. Madrigale per più 'caminantes' con Gidon Kremer* (1988)
Tape and ensemble	*Composizione per orchestra no. 2 – Diario polacco '58* (1965) *A floresta é jovem e cheja de vida* (1966) *Intolleranza 1960 Suite* (1969) *Musica-Manifesto no. 1: Un volto, del mare – Non consumiamo Marx* (1969)	*Como una ola de fuerza y luz* (1972) *Al gran sole carico d'amore (Fragments)* (1978)	*Das atmende Klarsein* (1981)
Stage works with tape	*Intolleranza 1960* (1961)	*Al gran sole carico d'amore* (1975)	

control for the composer. At Nono's disposal was a comprehensive selection of contemporary studio technologies, including nine oscillators and a variety of tape machines. Intending to extend the experiments in sound spatialisation already made by his mentor Hermann Scherchen, the four-track machine was of particular relevance to Nono as he worked on *Omaggio a Emilio Vedova*. On first listening, it's evident that the studio is new territory for Nono. With its deep, booming, metallic reverberations, dense, rhythmic layers and prepared piano-like percussive sonorities, *Omaggio* could almost be a piece of musique concrète from the previous decade or even earlier; however, the work is entirely composed from sine waves, manipulated by different types of modulation and filtering. Dedicated to his friend, the painter and former freedom fighter Emilio Vedova – who would later work with Nono on *Intolleranza 1960* – *Omaggio* allowed Nono to approach composition from a different perspective, experimenting and 'painting' with sound in the fluid way that is now familiar to anyone who composes on a DAW. Despite its technical limitations – by 1960 Stockhausen had already composed a plethora of considerably more complex electronic works – there are clear indications of Nono's future trajectory in the studio, which will feature booming, metallic sounds, a heavy use of reverb and a 'radio tuning' effect consisting of rapid shifts between material.[51] For Nono, this approach to composition eliminated one of Western music's fundamental dialectics, the dialectic between sound and notation. Interpretation was no longer necessary, the 'final' cut was on the tape; and yet, different playback machines, spatialisation and acoustic spaces do all effect how that 'final' cut sounds in performance, not to mention the decay of the medium itself over time. Nevertheless, as Impett (2019, p.197) comments, this new way of working 'presented Nono with an alternative map of his own thought, a new model for his own practice, that would persist'.

The improvisatory approach that studio composition encouraged resonated with earlier open-ended rehearsal and production techniques, from the theatre practice of Piscator to that of Nono's contemporary theatre-maker Joan Littlewood, while its reliance on editing techniques echoed the collision montage techniques of the Soviet film-maker Sergei Eisenstein. Two decades later, Nono was still experimenting in the studio, saying of his time at the SWR Experimental Studio: 'I begin with virtually no idea' (Prati, Masotti & Nono, 2018, p.311). Time spent in the studio also formed a decisive step in Nono's self-imposed gradual removal from the conventional, bourgeois concert scene, a scene that, unsurprisingly for a communist, he was increasingly ill at ease with. Electronics would allow Nono to incorporate acoustic materials taken

---

[51] As can be heard in *Omaggio* from c. 3:58 to 4:28, for example.

directly from the environment of the factory floor, in a creative programme dedicated to composing a music of and for working people and raising awareness of social and economic conditions in a similar way to that of Piscator during the 1920s. Even though *Omaggio* does not employ recording in the field, or use others' pre-existing recordings in the way that Cage did, it still functions hauntologically through its embrace of temporal and spatial rupture, deeply embedded in its working processes, its dedicatee, its use of technology, sound world and practical political ramifications. As Carla Henius (1991, p.76) recalled, 'his most convincing trait was his incredible seriousness about life, that is, his power to force utopias, the previously impossible, into reality' (my translation). Nono's next works would channel the creative affordances offered by tape into composing from and for real-life situations and audiences, while also addressing the justice that is yet to come, sought by all hauntology's ghosts.

While Nono was composing *Omaggio*, he was also working on *Intolleranza 1960*, a technologically rich work for the stage that takes capitalist bourgeois indifference to human suffering as its theme – especially that of the 'outsider', whether financial, geographical or political – and opposition to this 'intolerance' via the character of an impoverished immigrant's desire to return home, the challenging situations he encounters during his endeavours and the emerging consciousness that results from these experiences. The work was designated an *azione scenica*, rather than an opera, by Nono, implying that dramatic situations were substituted for linear narrative, rather in the style of the expressionist *Stationendrama* in its approach to narrative content and the juxtaposition of themes and situations to deliver a dramatic totality. Nono had already studied the works and practice of German and Russian left-wing creatives and dramaturgs, including Piscator, Toller, Eisenstein and Mayakovsky, and acknowledged the debt to Schoenberg's multimedia opera *Die Glückliche Hand* (1910–13) in his programme note for *Intolleranza*'s premiere (Impett, 2019, p.219). We have already seen how closely Piscator's dramatic practice resonates with hauntological concerns, and these same strategies would reappear in Nono's *Intolleranza*. Inspiration also came from the contemporary Czech theatre company *Laterna Magika*, who shared political ideals with Nono, and whose innovative use of multimedia – initially focused on the interaction between film and live performance – can be observed throughout *Intolleranza*. For the premiere, Nono collaborated with Emilio Vedova to produce a series of stark images that could be projected during the performance, much in the manner of Piscator's use of the projector in productions of *The Merchant of Berlin* and *Economic Competition* during the 1920s; Nono's mixing of live and recorded voices – made at the RAI – throughout the performance is also reminiscent of earlier dramatic models. Despite its broadly Marxist themes, Nono's use of technology, aesthetic-driven musical syntax and fragmentary structure resisted the contemporary formalist and socialist-realist conceptions of drama and music in the Soviet Union, and nearly every aspect of the production is involved in processes of decentring.

Hauntologically, *Intolleranza* foregrounds three areas: Nono's use of technology; textual and dramatic fragmentation and self-quotation. By utilising pre-recordings of the chorus and Vedova's projections, Nono was able to weave a complex fabric of decentred sound and image, enabling a double layer of commentary between the live and recorded action that explicitly overturns the sense of linear time, while increasing dramatic tension on the stage between the live and the 'once' live. Space too is decentred, emphasising the 'tele' not only through the use of recorded materials and live onstage voices, but also through speaker spatialisation within the auditorium, increasing the sense of fragmentation and disorientation present in text and situation. This technique is particularly noticeable in act 1, scene three, 'the demonstration', where, via four groups of speakers, Nono distributed the pre-recorded chorus across the stage, at the sides of the hall and behind the audience, thus fragmenting and decentring the orientation of sound and its sources. The 'medium of the media' is doubly foregrounded technologically, first through Nono's use of tape and Vedova's projections, and second through the projection of contemporary, and thus changing, media headlines – the more absurd the better – in the ballet section that opens the second act, along with a tape of quotidian absurdities. The disconnect between the action onstage and the deliberately inconsequential – although (presumably) factually accurate – journalistic content echo's Piscator's earlier theatrical practice, subtly reinforcing contemporary means of news and information dissemination and control in the West, while emphasising bourgeois indifference to the suffering of the working classes and dispossessed. Did Nono intend to imply that his audience was complicit in the protagonist's suffering, and that by consuming media banalities and observing situations of intolerance unfold on the safety of the stage that they are in fact as indifferent to 'intolerance' as the policemen in scene 4?[52] Nono remained critical of the media's role in shaping public consciousness and promotion of the arts, commenting in 1983:

> It is, ultimately, a question of power. The *media* focus on the 'famous', ... but technological research, new experiments and, still further, the serious problems of education: these are not even superficially touched upon. A country's musical state of affairs is not determined solely by the composer or his music, but from the totality of all these elements that then determine its progress or failure. (Prati, Masotti & Nono, 2018, p.315)

---

[52] B.A. Zimmermann exposes audience complicity when a searchlight is shone onto the audience in the final act of his opera *Die Soldaten* (1958–64, premiered 1965).

Fragmentation extends to Nono's choice of texts, comprising poetry and part of the original libretto by Angelo Ripellino,[53] with further content from Brecht, Éluard, Mayakovsky and Julius Fučík and reflections on human rights abuses in the Franco-Algerian conflict by Henri Alleg. The result is a panoply of agonised voices – policemen, political prisoners, demonstrators, miners, the protagonist, his lover and companion, refugees and victims of political torture – signifying the double identity of the group and the individual, all of whom are emblematic of hauntology's spectres, eternally waiting for the lost future of justice that is yet to come, relayed across fractured time, while haunting past, present and future. The same time constraints that forced him to radically adapt his libretto also had ramifications on his working process, with Nono eventually making quite extensive use of self-quotation, repurposing material from *Due espressioni* (1953), *Incontri* (1955) and *Il canto sospeso* (1955–56). Nono is literally mining his own past and integrating revenants, in the shape of fragmented ghosts of former pieces, into the present, in an echo of the double identity (group/ individual) played out by the characters. Illustrative of dialectics on many levels – live voices/recorded voices, live sounds/dead technology, political documentation/poetry, live singers/ghost singers, focused sound/spatialised sound – the looser style of compositional practice evident in *Intolleranza*, built on the more open-ended compositional process already nascent in *Omaggio*, and strategies of improvisation and experimentation similar to Piscator's working methods would become increasingly important in Nono's future projects.[54]

4.2 *La fabbrica illuminata:* The Factory of Death

Following the premiere of *Intolleranza*, Nono continued to build on the technologically enabled and socially relevant practice already trialled in that work, and a chance encounter with the poet Giuliano Scabia at the premiere would lead both to the genesis of *La fabbrica illuminata* and to the intervening project from which it grew, the unrealised *Un diario italiano*. Working on the premise that to be socially relevant, the arts must intervene rather than merely comment on social and political injustice, Nono and Scabia set about developing a model of flexible artistic plurality, encompassing elements of music, theatre and the visual arts in a mobile hierarchy, further supported by a rational, socially aware use of technology that enabled workers voices to be heard in their own terms, rather than being processed through the aegis of the 'academy'. Factory

---

[53] Despite successful early collaboration, ultimately Nono abandoned much of Ripellino's libretto due to time constraints and diverging creative priorities.
[54] Nono had contacted Piscator about the possible use of film in *Intolleranza*, and would formally collaborate with him on *Die Ermittlung* in 1965.

workers, union officials and others involved in the class struggle would work alongside the composer and ensemble, with their words and concrete environmental sounds used documentary style in the final artistic creation. Like Joan Littlewood, who stressed the importance of 'the absorption of the playwright into the collective' (Leach, 2006, p.163), Nono too envisioned a mode of working that was collective and ensemble-driven, distributing creative control more evenly throughout the group and using technology symbolically as well as materially. *Un diario italiano* combined historical and contemporary text materials ranging from poetry, documentary film and reportage to political documents and first-hand accounts of industrial action, factory conditions and instances of exploitation in Turin, Palermo and Venice. Although *Un diario*'s potential remained unfulfilled, Nono's conceptualisation of a multimedia stage work in six scenes with soloists, interspersed with four pre-recorded and spatialised choruses consisting of fragments of political and social textual content, clearly anticipates the hauntological, social and political basis of *La fabbrica illuminata*.

Dedicated to the workers at the Italsider steel plant in Genoa-Cornigliano, *La fabbrica illuminata*, for female voice and four-track magnetic tape, perfectly exemplifies not only Derrida's conception of hauntology but also later developments in the field by Fisher and others. In a similar manner to *Un diario*, elements of which are repurposed in *La fabbrica*, the text was composed by Giuliano Scabia, and drawn from several sources, including fragments of speech – slang, shouted orders and conversations – from the Italsider plant, excerpts from union publications, employment contracts and a quatrain from Cesare Pavese's *Due poesie a T*. Nono's use of documentary media materials aligns the work with hauntological concerns, and even though *La fabbrica* is based on one specific factory, the object of the factory – the industrial production of steel – takes place in such an overwhelmingly hostile, alien and incomprehensible environment, especially to those outside the industry, that the 'tele' applies as much to the listening experience of most audiences as to factory automation processes and Nono's use of recording technology. The title's 'illumination' refers principally to the practice of shiftwork, referenced in section 3: *Giro del letto*, demanded by the Italsider plant's constant operation, where its employees worked in artificial 'daylight' at all times, but this 'illumination' could equally reference the glare of molten steel reported by the workers to Scabia, and incorporated into the tape part – 'workers' exposure to accidental falls, to blinding light, to high-voltage current' (Cossettini, 2010, p. xxxvi) – or the watchfulness of management, as exemplified by the 'time and motion study'.

Nono, Scabia and Marino Zuccheri – the sound technician from RAI – visited the factory for three days of discussion with the workers and recording the factory's acoustic environment. Nono recorded the workers and the plant's overall sonic landscape, gathering a considerable quantity of auditory documentation, including workers' voices, the blast furnaces, steel pouring and other manufacturing processes. This process of sonic documentation allows the recording equipment to act as a conduit through which the auditory confrontation between workers and machinery, men and metal, workers and management flows, while also symbolising the overarching dynamic of money and power that drives the capitalist economic model of which the factory is a constituent part. Far from delivering the jet packs, labour-saving devices and endless leisure that the 'lost future' of the Italsider plant – and others like it – appeared to promise during the heady optimism of the 1960s, the reality was an environment where surplus labour exploitation and a shocking lack of industrial safety proliferated. Increased automation did not improve working conditions, it only led to higher unemployment and lower wages for those still in work. Nono's pluralistic use of audio documentation allowed the workers not only to experience their everyday environment from a new perspective, but also to reflect, sonically, on the 'justice yet to come' of their employment situation, in effect, a sonic 'archive' acting as a pledge to the future. The workers later commented: 'Listening to this music composed with our sounds-noises and with our words, we become aware of our alienated state in the factory. We work like mechanized robots, almost no longer realizing the violence of the human sound situation. Now we are rediscovering it and recovering awareness of it even through music' (Nono, 2018c, p.281). The concept of workers as 'mechanized robots' raises further questions concerning hauntology, through the agency/non-agency of the revenant. Not only does 'mechanized' imply repetitive actions, but, as Derrida writes concerning the complexities of speaking with ghosts in *Archive Fever*, 'A phantom speaks . . . this means that without responding it disposes of a response, a bit like the answering machine whose voice outlives its moment of recording: you call, the other person is dead, now, whether you know it or not, and the voice responds to you . . .' (Derrida, 1996, p.62) – mechanisation also encompasses a dialogue between the living and the dead that overturns the spatial and temporal. As listeners, we 'activate' *La fabbrica*, but the work also elicits a response from *us*. Through Nono's agency, the workers have been transformed into sonic ghosts. Fixed for eternity, as revenants that still respond every time *La fabbrica* is heard even though they do not 'speak' as such.

From the beginning of the project, Nono was insistent that *La fabbrica* should take into account the 'psycho-physical reactions of the workers rather than merely "photograph" them while they worked in the factory . . . it is not a work to be analyzed superficially' (Garavaglia & Nono, 2018, p.256), with the separate elements of the piece fabricated into a fully integrated understanding of the factory workers lived experience 'not . . . a mere collage of sounds and noises' (Garavaglia & Nono, 2018, p.257). As an example of hauntology in action from both political and sonic perspectives, Nono's rather focused – or limited, depending on the point of view – sonic palette and studio processes work to advantage in the attempt to humanise and archive the factory experience. Nono's fluid, agile, even intuitive approach in the studio allows for a 'real-time' sense of the urgency of the steel plant, its inherent dangers and the inexorable nature of work in such an environment.

La fabbrica illuminata consists of four episodes of material, distributed over three parts and a finale. Its final form and content were realised after processes of improvisation and collaboration between Nono and the creative collective, consisting of Zuccheri, the Italsider workers, Scabia, the RAI choir and the soloist Carla Henius. The four episodes are:

Part I
1. *Coro iniziale* [*Corale I, II, III & IV*] (soloist, recorded RAI choirs)
2. Tape solo (factory noises, workers' voices)

Part II
3. *Giro del letto* (Circling the Bed) (soloist, recording of Henius, electronic material)

Part III
4. *Tutta la città* (soloist, recording of Henius, chorus), and *Finale* (soloist)

Nono (2018b, p.354) described Henius as 'using her voice's wide range of articulations' in passages of unpredictable improvisation. Split across four tracks, Henius's improvisation was tracked onto other examples of her voice, coupled with electronic materials, 'unifying the recorded and the live parts – mingling with fragments of workers' recorded voices – with fragments of the RAI-Milan chorus' (Nono, 2018b) in a complex process of sonic re-elaboration, rather than simplistic audio documentation. Henius recalled that:

> a quarter of a year of incredible joint work followed [her acceptance of Nono's offer] in the Studio di Fonologia in Milan or Venice, and it was a completely different kind of work to that in *Intolleranza*. There was nothing left to interpret, but I was actually a kind of material with which Nono composed and played. What I provided were mosaic pieces, of which he rejected perhaps 9/10 of what was produced and what was left he really 'composed' in the literal sense. It was a completely different kind of interpretation that was expected of the singer, the performer, because – like with

a stroboscope – it allowed the most diverse feelings to follow one another without any connection. We sometimes felt it was a kind of inner monologue like Joyce. (Henius, 1991, pp.79–80, my translation)

Always, the tensions between the live and recorded – the soloist and choirs and workers, the mechanised and living – are present in Nono's Piscator-like sonic theatre, and like the protagonist from *Intolleranza*, the soloist's isolated voice can be thought of as symbolic of both the individual and the group. As the opening line of text emphasises – 'factory of death they called it' – the workers words, their recorded voices and their environment are revenants, and like all Derrida's 'ghosts', they await reparation, each voice yielding to another. Despite the revenant's hoped-for more equal society, the tape part itself is more ambivalent. Does it, in fact, symbolise the 'fabbrica dei morti la chiamavano / factory of death they called it' where the workers are trapped on its magnetic surface in endlessly repeating loops of labour that are gradually erased as the iron oxide decays? The future implied by the tape seems much more uncertain even than Pavese's final quatrain: 'the morning will pass / the anguish will fade / it will not be this way forever / you will recover something' (Cossettini, 2010, p.xxxvi). Exponentially increased, this uncertainty will be revisited twice more in *Die Ermittlung* (The Investigation) (1965), incidental music for Peter Weiss's play of the same name, and *Ricorda cosa ti hannno fatto in Auschwitz* (1966). In both works, Nono uses two direct quotes from *La fabbrica illuminata* – 'fabbrica dei morti / factory of death' and 'fabbrica come lager / factory like a concentration camp' – to draw clear parallels between his experience of industrial conditions in the Italian steel industry during the 1950s and 1960s, and the industrialised efficiency of Nazi genocide. Postperformance, the Italsider workers invited Nono to discuss the work with them in greater deal, and Nono was struck by the technical detail of their questions. Nono recalled,

> They asked me to prepare better because they wanted to know the technical process of my work precisely. Those workers did not stop . . . at the fideistic, party line, ideological element, but, showing very high cognitive intelligence not affected by a humanistic cultural bias, they were interested . . . in the technical data that for them was the only analytical and critical yardstick (Garavaglia & Nono, 2018, p.256).

The workers, operating in a highly mechanised and technical industry themselves, were particularly interested by Nono's analysis of 'the relationship between the "natural" material recorded in the factory and the artificial, electrically generated material with all possible transformations implemented at various times' (Garavaglia & Nono, 2018, p.257).

Nono had always intended different set-ups depending on the occasion: the concert version for solo voice and quadraphonic tape; the radio version for monophonic tape, with the solo voice included; and for other public venues, such as lectures and cultural centres, a version for quadraphonic tape, again with the voice incorporated. The use of tape provides not only spatialisation for the chorus but also a concomitant temporalisation of the recorded materials, allowing the live and 'present' vocal soloist to dialogue with the 'tele' recorded elements. Time is most definitely out of joint in *La fabbrica*, and the nature of magnetic tape, subject to processes of audible decay, further emphasises this, as does the evolution of the storage and dissemination formats for performance. From the original quadraphonic tapes to a DVD with wav. files that is included with the current Ricordi edition of the score, the traces of the original tapes remain – the ghosts live on. Another instance of time out of joint can be heard in the juxtaposition of what, for 1964, was still a relatively new medium – tape – placed alongside a much older musical model, the four-section cantata. As Nono ruefully admitted in an interview with Bernd Leukert (1974): 'There's another thing I understood too late: the form of *La fabbrica* is the form of a Bach cantata [. . .] it was constructed that way by me and by the workers, but then I realised ever more clearly that it's based on a Bach cantata' (Cossettini, 2010, p.xxi).

Hauntologically, *La fabbrica* can be considered in four principal and complementary ways:

1. Electronically recorded archives of factory sounds and music performed by the RAI chorus emphasising the 'medium of the media' and 'tele-techno-iconicity' in a sound world that is able to refer beyond itself, into wider political and cultural arenas.
2. Electronically generated material, incorporating free improvisation by mezzo-soprano Carla Henius, and other synthesised sounds. These are combined and 'electronically modified often beyond recognition' (Cossettini, 2010, p.xxi).
3. Performance history, particularly pertaining to the changing technological formats necessary for performance and dissemination, and the ever-present danger of obsolescence. For example, the DVD format of the current edition is much less easily accessible than it was only ten years ago.
4. Politics. Nono's process of sonic re-elaboration takes audio documentation and transforms it into an art object specifically for the workers – as 'co-researchers' – at the Italsider plant, in a way that is comprehensible and relevant. However, underlying this utopian aim is Derrida's 'techno-tele-discursivity', implying the collection of accepted or hegemonic norms from

a particular period, all at the service of the 'techno-tele'. In other words, despite Nono's idealistic intentions, the beast of capital is always present.

La fabbrica functions conceptually somewhat in the way of a grid, in that every instance of documentation, and each fragment of recorded and poetic text, is both linked and yet stands alone. Although there is structure, there is the impression of constant movement – temporal and spatial – while the concept of 'centre' is rejected, making *La fabbrica* a testament to both past and future. Derrida (1986, pp.70, 73) explains:

> The meaning of 'grid' does not achieve assembled totality. It crosses through. To establish a grid is to cross through, to go through a channel. It is the experience of permeability. . . . Such crossing does not move through an already existing-texture; it weaves this texture, it invents the histological structure of a text, of what one would call in English a 'fabric'.

The portability of the four-track tape system and the multiple performance arrangements Nono had developed allowed for great flexibility of dissemination. It was as easy to perform *La fabbrica* for a workers' collective as it was to broadcast it on the radio, and even live performances were relatively uncomplicated to set up; thus the collective financial power of the music industry, as represented by concert venues and management, has been reduced by the agency of hauntology's ghostly medium – tape.

4.3 Fragments and Revenants: *Die Ermittlung* and *Ricorda cosa ti hanno fatto in Auschwitz*

> The *revenant* is going to come . . . everything begins in the imminence of a *re-apparition* . . .
>
> – Jacques Derrida, *Spectres of Marx*[55]

As the 1960s progressed, the use of fragmentation, pre-recorded and processed materials and the repurposing of extracts from earlier works in hybrid forms that combined live sounds, taped sounds and electronically generated sounds became increasingly common, paving the way for Nono's practice during the 1970s. *Die Ermittlung* – the title of Nono's music composed to accompany the play of the same name by Peter Weiss (1965) – utilised vocal, instrumental and electronic sound sources, and incorporated fragments of several earlier works; it also finally gave Nono the opportunity to work with Erwin Piscator in person. Having first met Piscator in 1954, Nono later recalled: 'I suddenly found myself in the presence of one of the figures who had most inspired my imagination' (Restagno, 2018, p.73). Already an admirer of Weiss's work, Nono was delighted to accept Piscator's

---

[55] Derrida, 2006, p.2.

invitation to contribute to his production of *Die Ermittlung*, the collaboration bringing together two high-profile practitioners of hauntology on the stage for the first time.

Weiss's *Die Ermittlung* is a courtroom-set dramatic situation that probes the shameful contract between German big business – including I. G. Farben, whose iron-oxide-coated tape had revolutionised sound recording – and the Holocaust, via materials gathered from the Frankfurt Auschwitz Trial of 1963–65, at which Weiss was an observer. The play is a searing indictment of rampant profiteering from the Nazi regime's industrial machinery of mass killing, and an unequivocally anti-fascist work, pointing an accusatory finger at the contemporary West German government's failings to root out fascism within West German society, in particular from the judiciary and the apparatus of government where many former members of the Nazi party were safely employed, thanks to a series of amnesties brought in after the war. It's hardly surprising that Weiss's play was embroiled in an East versus West debate from the outset, one in which Nono was happy to participate. The world premiere(s) took place simultaneously in twelve theatres, across West and East German cities, with a further premiere taking place in London by the Royal Shakespeare Company. The work is subtitled 'Oratorio in Eleven Cantos', and its thirty-three-part structure – eleven cantos divided into three scenes each – follows that of Dante Alighieri's *Divine Comedy*, with each canto alternating anonymous witness statements against the response of a named defendant. Acting as a central focus for Nono and Piscator, the fifth and sixth cantos concentrate on named individuals: Lili Tofler and SS Corporal Stark. As a whole, the play is open-ended, stopping before the trial verdicts are relayed, effectively offering an endless 'now' of testimony. Much of the text material is taken verbatim from the trial, relating the journey of the victims from their first arrival at the concentration camp to their ultimate destination, the gas chamber and crematorium, while relaying an increasingly horrifying and violent catalogue of incidents along the way, as though on a journey into hell.

Piscator took a very studied approach to the direction of his production at the Berlin Freie Volksbühne, rejecting any use of film, projection or other documentary material, thus avoiding any possible accusations of utilising 'manipulated propaganda' for contemporary East versus West ideological battles (Nielinger-Vakil, 2015, p.127). Thus, the documentary and hauntological content of *Die Ermittlung* was supplied by Weiss's use of verbatim documentation from the Auschwitz trial, described by Nono (2018a, pp.230–31) as embodying 'the conflict and the superimposition between present and past, between memory, testimony, and current reality', as well as Nono's reuse of his own earlier recorded compositional materials. Nono's task was daunting: to compose music that could 'represent the six million dead – those who could no longer speak out' (Nielinger-Vakil, 2015, p.128). Eventually consisting of many small fragments, as with *La fabbrica illuminata*, Nono initially focused on the sounds of the human voice, as chorus or soloist, restricted to women's and children's voices – a conception that Piscator also shared – to best represent the human tragedy unfolding on the stage. To this end, Nono recorded some original material at the Studio Fonologia in Milan, as well as utilising recordings of the children's choir of the Piccolo Teatro di Milano,[56] the soprano Stephania Woytowitcz (from 1959),[57] and excerpts from *Cori di Didone* and *'Ha venido'*. *Canciones para Silvia*, but all 'deprived of the semantic element of a literary text' (Nono, 2018a, p.234). Nono then added instrumental recordings – for brass and woodwind instruments – including parts of *Diario polacco '58* and *Il canto sospeso*, together with a panoply of electronic and tape content from the studio. As with so much of Nono's composition, especially tape-based, the sonic palette reverberates with metallic sounds – both blown and struck – in combination with the human voice. To these principal sonorities are added percussive electronic interjections and concrete sonic materials to indicate the rushing of gas, heard in 'Canto 10, Zyklon B', and flames, in 'Canto 11, The Fire-Ovens', while reverberation, filtration and transposition are evident throughout. Noise is a prominent feature, increasingly so as the drama progresses, echoing hauntology's foregrounding of media distortion and disintegration. Perhaps one of the most disturbing vocal sonorities in the play is that of laughter, particularly prominent in the sixth canto, 'SS Corporal Stark', and the eighth, 'Phenol'. Every time there is laughter onstage, Nono responds with silence; it is hard to imagine any other response that would be appropriate after, for example, the detailed description of the murder of children in Canto 8.[58]

Nono in his conception rejected any hint of a programmatic approach to Weiss's play, stating that 'I was not interested in a solution involving incidental music' (Nono, 2018a, p.229). Nono was also aware of the heavy responsibility of his task, observing: 'Piscator saw the music-theater relationship correctly: that what neither the word nor the stage was able to express and represent, the music had to do. The millions of dead in the concentration camps' (Nono, 2018, p.232). Of great interest to Nono was the Berlin Volksbühne's sophisticated speaker array, comprising tape recorders connected to 'numerous loudspeakers placed all around (right, left, onstage, on the ceiling) and . . . a loudspeaker also in a space under the floor of the hall right under the audience'. Utilising this equipment, it was possible to make the floor and audience tremble, enabling 'an acoustic-musical opportunity for emotional involvement greater than anyone could imagine' (Restagno, 2018, p.74). The physicality of Nono and Piscator's sound

---

[56] Impett (2019, p.255) suggests that this was originally part of *Un diario Italiano*.
[57] Possibly for *Diario polacco '58* (Nielinger-Vakil, 2015, p.133).
[58] Laughter occurs onstage in Canto 1, Canto 6 (twice) and Canto 8.

spatialisation, especially at such low levels (sub-woofer style), elicits an empathetic response from the audience that would be difficult to provoke using other means. Sound thrusts the audience full centre, reinforcing the sense of kinship with the survivors that Piscator was intending. As Derrida comments in *Specters of Marx* (2006, p.202), 'to haunt does not mean to be present'; *Die Ermittlung* underlines the lack of 'presence' through the distance of time (the twenty years between the end of the war and the Auschwitz trials), through media (Nono's use of tape, in part as materialised memory; Weiss' use of verbatim trial reports) and through the simulacra of events presented in the theatre itself. The victims may now be 'virtual', or ghostly, 'with the spectre understood . . . as that which acts without (physically) existing' (Fisher, 2014, p.18); but although they can only seek justice as ghostly revenants, the survivors can demand reparation in the present, using memory and testimony to haunt the guilty and wider society. As Fisher observes: 'Hauntology is the proper temporal mode for a history made up of gaps, erased names and sudden abductions . . . the fragments of a time permanently out of joint' (Fisher, 2014, p.130).

Nono's engagement with the subject matter of *Die Ermittlung* – the legacy of Auschwitz and the violence of fascist oppression – would continue, its subsequent manifestation being an autonomous work, repurposing the sound materials already used for *Die Ermittlung*, called *Ricorda cosa ti hanno fatto in Auschwitz* (Remember what they did to you in Auschwitz). As a philosophy of revenants and ghosts, hauntology is closely aligned with the word 'remember', implying the 'tele' of the past, collective inheritance, the anticipation of its inevitable reappearance and the desire for justice: 'The *revenant* is going to come . . . everything begins in the imminence of a *re*-apparition . . .' (Derrida, 2006, p.2). The title was probably inspired by Alberto Nirenstajn's 1958 account of the Warsaw ghetto and the Polish resistance, *Ricorda cosa ti ha fatto Amalek*, a copy of which was in Nono's possession. Although there is no new material, the structure is quite different from the earlier work, replacing extreme fragmentation with a more through-composed approach, while condensing or eliminating other materials. *Ricorda cosa ti hanno fatto in Auschwitz* consists of three unequal sections: (1) Canto del lager (Canto of the camp); (2) Canto della fine di Lilli Tofler (Canto of the death of Lili Tofler) and (3) Canto della possibilità di sopravvivere (Canto of the possibility of survival). Although the links to Weiss's play are clear, the music here takes on a much more direct mode of expression, wherein, as Nanni (2006, p.51) notes, 'the music itself is an outcry both of desperation and at the same time of accusation'. Memory, inheritance, legacy; in *Ricorda*'s sound world, these hauntological concepts speak to the possibility of survival and even of justice, for, as Hägglund suggests, without memory, there can be no justice. Derrida (2006, p.67) notes that, 'like all inheritors, we are in mourning', and while most mourn for the victims of oppression, for their suffering, the loss of life and the slow pace of justice, there is a sinister flipside, for there are those who will always mourn for the loss of the Reich and its ideals.

4.4 A floresta é jovem e cheja de vida and Contrappunto dialettico alla mente

> ... traditional language does not work anymore.
> – Nono in 'Autobiography Recounted by Enzo Restagno'[59]

The 1960s proved to be a period of frenetic activity for Nono, both politically and compositionally, with works for solo tape, tape and ensemble and tape and the stage being produced in rapid succession, and compositional practice dominated by field recording and hauntological concepts very much to the fore. Moving from the memorial specificity of *Die Ermittlung* and *Ricorda cosa ti hanno fatto in Auschwitz*, evidence of Nono's increasingly international political engagement can be seen in both *A floresta é jovem e cheja de vida* and *Contrappunto dialettico alla mente*, with both works tackling global themes – the war in Vietnam,[60] the fight for independence from colonial control across Africa, and racial discrimination in the United States – while also addressing more generalised concerns of the class struggle, labour relations and the fight against imperialist and right-wing oppression. Made in collaboration with the writer Giovanni Pirelli, *A floresta é jovem e cheja de vida* (The forest is young and full of life) was a continuation of earlier developments made by Nono in his expanding conception of music theatre. As with *fabbrica*, the composition makes extensive use of documentary materials, and utilises processes where spatial and temporal decentring are consistently foregrounded. Much of the performance content – both live and taped – was arrived at after periods of workshopping and improvisation with the interpreters and in the studio, both of these facets resonating with the work processes of Piscator. It's also worthy of note that, except for the percussion parts, Nono did not produce a score for *A floresta*, instead relying on the commitment and integrity of his original performers and the recording made by the same ensemble, placing the final 'scripted' tape in hauntological dialogue with the 'unscripted' live interpreters.

On multiple levels, the ghostly dominates *A floresta* and many subsequent works. This ghostliness operates on three main levels: (1) the 'no longer',

---

[59] Restagno, 2018, p.81.
[60] In another example of temporal instability, Nono continued his engagement with Vietnam in *Al gran sole carico d'amore*, an engagement with nineteenth- and twentieth-century history, through a non-narrative, situation-derived structure, composed of multilayered and collaged text fragments drawn from multiple genres. The other two situations are the Paris Commune and the Russian Revolution.

embodied by the voices of the dead, trapped as sonic reverberations by Nono, endlessly repeating; (2) the 'not yet', evidenced by the voices of the living and the dead and their search for justice, equality and change – it's the principal reason why ghosts 'haunt' after all – and the texts, where Nono collates a hauntological archaeology, from political speeches and pamphlets that ultimately did not achieve their aims (the 'no longer' and 'not yet'), to contemporary protest slogans and song lyrics that reinforce the temporal and spatial decentring of the first text group and (3) collaboration with living poets and dramatists, where new work is generated, but in the service of ghosts.

A large portion of the tape part had originally been conceived as a different work – *Escalation*[61] – written for, and with, the artists of the Living Theatre, an experimental US theatre group, co-led by a former Piscator disciple, Judith Malina. Nono utilised filtering and ring modulation to create a storm of voices, with the rest of the tape consisting of more material from the Living Theatre – the opening of *Frankenstein* (after Shelley) and improvised 'jungle' evocations – combined with Nono's field recordings of peace demonstrations in the United States during 1965. Nono's choice of documentary materials is wide-ranging, resulting in something of a global political manifesto. Text sources – all of them documentary – fall into three main categories: (1) African decolonisation – Frantz Fanon, Patrice Lumumba and the Angolan freedom fighter Gabriel, whose words form the title; (2) Caribbean and Central America – Fidel Castro, Pedro Duno and (3) Vietnam – Nguyen Van Troi. Further political content is derived from American and Italian protest movements, while, to underline Nono's political stance, especially in American eyes, the work was dedicated to the National Liberation Front of Vietnam. The eventual forces for the premiere consisted of soprano (Liliana Poli), three actors (Kadigia Bove, Elena Vicini and Berto Troni), clarinet (William O. Smith), percussion ensemble – playing five dramatically lit bronze plates – and two four-channel tapes.

A floresta engages with hauntological strategies in four principal areas: (1) its use of recorded media (four-track tapes) as emblematic of tele-techno-iconicity and tele-techno-discursivity; (2) its role in decentring the voice, through fragmentation and phonemes, and politically, through the voicing of global anti-Western capitalist ideologies; (3) its engagement with the media as both purveyor of orthodoxy and suppression of non-orthodox narratives, and as a means of disseminating dissenting voices, through documentation of first-person narratives, political manifestos, and group protest and (4) its engagement with revenants in all the above, and particularly through the voices of the murdered and

---

[61] Based on military strategist and advisor to the US Department of Defence Herman Kahn's highly controversial article 'Escalation as a Strategy' from *Fortune* magazine (April 1965) (Impett, 2019, p.262).

suppressed. Woven through *A floresta* are the twin threads of the revenant's desire for a justice yet to come, coupled with – in this case – the implied imperial fear should any such eventuality be reached. Temporally, Africa and Vietnam are still waiting for justice, still deeply embroiled in the struggle for freedom, while Cuba has achieved a measure of success in the present, looking to the future for stability and autonomy without outside interference. It is the human voice – amplified and spatialised – that dominates *A floresta*, its emotional immediacy used to relay words from diverse linguistic traditions that are both spatially and temporally 'out of joint', as live and recorded sound merge into a total sound field.

Continuing *A floresta*'s, themes of global class struggle and US policies of imperial oppression, and using almost the same forces, although restricted to tape without live performance interventions, *Contrappunto dialettico alla mente* (1968) places racial discrimination at its heart, using as a framing device Sonia Sanchez's words on the assassination of Malcolm X and an anti-Vietnam War manifesto ('Black Women Enraged') by a Harlem-based African American women's group (Rizzardi, 2006, p.55). Described as 'an inextricable interpenetration of old and new components' (Restagno, 2018, p.83), *Contrappunto* is one of Nono's relatively few settings of avant-garde poetry, with Nanni Balestrini's words being placed in the context of a structural, musical parody inspired by Adriano Banchieri's (1608) comic and highly inventive *Festino nella sera del giovedì grasso avanti cena*, in a similar juxtaposition of disparate centuries to those of *Al gran sole carico d'amore* in the following decade. Dedicated to Denis Bravo, leader of the Venezuelan Armed Front for National Liberation, political dissent and decentring are clearly articulated, but Nono's conception of *Contrappunto* as a radiophonic work[62] is also indicative of a collective and democratic approach to dissemination and reception, where the imagined hauntological signature of the medium – static – reinforces Nono's compositional 'tuning' between his diverse selection of documented materials, live performance and generative studio practice.

From the beginning, Nono is playing with time that is out of joint: contemporary poetry and politics are placed within a setting inspired by the seventeenth-century Venetian comic madrigal tradition, while also combining field recordings with studio-generated materials. The titular dialectic thus not only juxtaposes opposing temporalities but also contrasts serious political content with semi-absurdist wordplay, the lyrical with the mundane and, as with so many of Nono's works, the individual and the group. Nono made extensive use of linguistic parody over the work's six sections, while

---

[62] Originally conceived for eight-track tape and corresponding speakers, the eventual format was stereophonic diffusion via radio. The change to stereo broadcast meant that no further spatialisation was required by the composer (Rizzardi, 2006, p.56).

his field recordings continue the theme of temporal – and spatial – juxtaposition, consisting of sounds from Venice's Rialto market, the Venetian lagoon and the lowest bell in the tower of St Mark's; and in the Studio di Fonologia, Nono recorded actors Kadigia Bove and Elena Vicini, the classically trained singer Liliana Poli and the RAI-Rome chorus in a process of 'adding-subtracting, composing-discomposing' (Nono, 2018b, p.355), delivering highly fragmented portions of word polyphony – including 'White House', 'Johnson' and 'Pentagon' – and other vocal effects[63] that result in periods of what Impett (2019, p.284) calls 'sonic pandemonium'. Metal sheets and pipes were manipulated in numerous ways to create a panoply of effects, 'filtered, superimposed, and "composed" with different time relationships among themselves' (Nono, 2018b, p.355). The recorded sounds fall into various categories: metal resonances; electronic modalities, and related tape manipulation procedures; spatially situated materials that evoke Venice's history as a great medieval and Renaissance trading centre and wielder of imperial power, and its role in historical economic and racial oppression. Placed in conjunction with contemporary, albeit fragmented, text materials, the entire work constantly plays back and forth through time, the legacy and revenants of Venice's past ricocheting off current arenas of injustice and conflict. As with *La fabbrica illuminata* (and its dedication to the workers of the Italsider steelworks), *Contrappunto*'s dialectic was considered sufficiently controversial politically – to US and Italian diplomatic sensibilities – to cause the work to be withdrawn from the 1968 Prix Italia.

4.5 The Late 1960s and the Move Towards Electronics

The close of the decade was a period of summation and transition, with the vast majority of tape works aligning with hauntological themes. Nono's style and working practices were well established, and clear trajectories concerning politics, the composer-performer interface, studio language, the use of documentary materials, and studio techniques are evident in *Musica-Manifesto no. 1: Un volto, del mare – Non consumiamo Marx* (1969), *Musiche per Manzù* (1969), *Como una ola de fuerza y luz* (1972) and *Für Paul Dessau* (1974). The 1970s was also a decade of change, with techniques already prefiguring the move to electronics in the 1980s and a more personal approach to content, as demonstrated in *Como una ola de fuerza y luz* and . . . . . *Sofferte onde serene . . .* (1976), where friendship and loss both come under scrutiny. Nono's working practices, based on close interaction with his interpreters, through improvisation and detailed co-research in the studio, continued during the 1970s. *Non consumiamo*, for soprano, actress and

---

[63] Such as speaking, whispering, singing, shouting and growling.

tape, saw Nono work with favoured collaborators Poli and Bove again, as well as the actress Edmonda Aldini. His close scrutiny of the human voice, achieved through periods of experimentation and improvisation – covering vocal articulation, timbre, range, and microphone placements – with his performers, anticipates the analytical approach to the piano that Nono would adopt in *Como una ola de fuerza y luz*, also featuring the soprano Slavka Taskova, and . . . . . *Sofferte onde serene* . . . with Maurizio Pollini as soloist. Although not a performer as such – except for some piano experiments in the studio for *Sofferte* – Nono's relationship with studio technician Marino Zuccheri remained a vital one, and Nono's reliance on experimentation and performer co-research as fundamental composing strategies ally his processes with those of Piscator, underlining the interconnected history of Marxist artistic creation.

Sonorities during this period continue Nono's focus on resonance, particularly relating to metal (brass, percussion and piano) and air (voices, brass and, to a lesser extent, woodwinds) coupled with studio processes that evoke a sense of spatial and temporal vastness. Thus, *Non consumiamo Marx* sees the reuse of the bells of St Mark's and recordings of metal tubes and sheets made with Stefania Woytowitcz the previous decade, and *Como una ola* features the mid and lower registers of the piano (metal) and the soprano voice (breath), both live and on the central tape part. *Musiche per Manzù* – composed to accompany Mario Bernardo's *Pace e Guerra*, a film study of the reconstruction of Rotterdam's Sint Laurenskerk, with particular focus on sculptor Giacomo Manzù's bronze doors – is dominated by the sounds of metal and air; again, one of the bells of St Mark's is reused, as is material from *Ricorda cosa ti hanno fatto in Auschwitz*, and choral voices (breath). The overall effect is of a giant resonating metal shell, articulated by air currents, processed at an ultra-slow tempo, which in many ways both shares and anticipates the endless 'now' of the Caretaker's *Theoretically Pure Anterograde Amnesia* (2006), a totemic work for twenty-first-century hauntology. *Für Paul Dessau* revisits fragments of earlier works – *Il canto sospeso*, *Non consumiamo Marx* and *Como una ola* – within a skilful amalgam of words, noise and music. Brass, bells and piano (metal) sonorities are evident throughout, while breath is present in both speech and choral singing. The overall effect is like a circle of radios, tuning in and out of range and amplitude – although static is not a prominent feature – rather in the manner of Stockhausen's *Telemusik* (1966) and *Hymnen* (1966–67).

Where political content is overt, imported documentation is a central focus, delivered through spoken texts – read by their original orators or by actors in the studio – and field recordings of protest events and political gatherings, presented in a sonic blend where past and present continually interpenetrate. Nono's predilection for self-quotation can also be viewed in this light; to quote the self is a political act in itself, in an intermingling of past events and future aspirations. It also underlines the deeply hauntological nature of Nono's work practice per se, where each piece emerges from another, fragments are recast and the incomplete or abandoned are given a new voice in different contexts. Nono mines his own past constantly, and the desire to 'rebuild' using old materials is of course as political as its obverse, the desire to destroy, a dialectic that is very evident in *Musiche per Manzù*. Tape and text emphasise how Derridean techo-tele-discursivity and iconicity are implicit strategies for Nono (the 'techno' of tele-techno), haunting these works temporally and spatially. Nono's texts, whether poetry, political speech, shouted slogan or manifesto, all interact with each other; thus in *Non consumiamo Marx*, in part 1 ('Un volto, e dal mare'), poetry by Pavese operates in dialectic with part 2's ('Non consumiamo Marx') field recordings of protests at the Venice Biennale and spoken political slogans from the Parisian demonstrations of 1968. The tele is further underlined by Nono's skilful deployment of spatialisation (fore/mid/background) and amplitude in the recordings. Emblematic of the ongoing class struggle, Impett (2019, p.296) considers this work to be Nono's 'most explicit engagement with contemporary events'. The title's reference to Marx connects the listener to past, present and future – also resonating with Derrida's still-to-be-written text – while dialectics (past/present, individual/group, poetry/politics, live/recorded and generated/retrieved) provide further modes of connection between parts 1 and 2. The dialectic is even extended to the original playing formats – 10″ vinyl EP and the 12″ LP reissue – with part 1 on side A and part 2 on side B.

A similarly overt approach to political content occurs in *Für Paul Dessau*. Contemporary expressions regarding global justice and freedom are combined with earlier manifestos; hence, Castro, Lenin, Guevara and Lumumba rub shoulders in a meta-manifesto of the living and the dead, and as a further manifestation of the revenant's desire for justice that is still to come. And yet there is a sense of timelessness, of time that is standing still, as the fragmented babble of voices blends into an eternal 'now', a spectral 'moment'. That fragmented babble is also redolent of the digital looping and sampling that will become prominent in music during the next decade. Conversation with the past and its politics can equally operate in the form of memory and lament, as demonstrated in *Como una ola*, where reflection on the life of Luciano Cruz, Chilean revolutionary and personal friend of Nono, is presented across a five-movement history of loss, memory, political action and eventual hope, conveyed by piano, soprano voice, orchestra and tape.

4.6 Spectral Moments: Tape in the 1980s

By the late 1970s Nono was increasingly looking to expand the sense of suspended time that is already apparent in *Musiche per Manzù*, *Für Paul Dessau* and ..... *Sofferte onde serene* .... Derrida (2006, p.xix) refers to such instances of suspended time as 'a spectral moment, a moment that no longer belongs to time, if one understands by this word the linking of modalized presents (past present, actual present: "now", future present)'. These instances of suspended time appear to no longer function as part of a traditional temporal narrative, but instead to reverberate as echoes, as 'a trace of which life and death would themselves be but traces and traces of traces' (Derrida, 2006, p.xx). Ghostly or not, although the moment is spectral, it is not any less real for that. It is still a moment of connection between performers, listeners and composer, while for Derrida, as hauntology is irreducible, such ghosts of futures past do not emanate from one point, place or time, but from the collective that is time out of joint. Nono's final work with tape, *La lontananza nostalgica utopica futura* is suffused with this sense of suspended, disjointed time, composed of lost futures and decaying memory, but also holding within itself distant utopias of a future yet to come. With the Milan studio in decline by the early 1980s, Nono would soon move his researches to the Experimental Studio of the Heinrich Strobel Foundation in Freiburg, where he was particularly inspired by the new Halaphon, a device for spatialising sound that would prove instrumental during the composition of *La lontananza nostalgica utopica futura*.

The phrase 'Caminantes, no hay caminos, hay que caminar' (Wanderer, there are no paths, yet you must walk), which Nono observed on a monastery wall in Toledo during a visit in 1985, inspired no fewer than four late works, including his final completed composition and his last and most ambitious work with magnetic tape, *La lontananza nostalgica utopica futura. Madrigale per piu 'Caminantes' con Gidon Kremer* (The nostalgic utopian future distance: madrigal for several 'travellers' with Gidon Kremer), for violin, eight tapes and eight to ten music stands, to which the quote is fundamental.[64] Nono had already established the notion of the 'traveller' through his increasingly complex designs for sound spatialisation in previous pieces, and this feature would become central to *La lontananza's* realisation, with the soloist physically moving throughout the performance – hence, the number of music stands specified, two of which, significantly, remain empty – and the sound technician electronically moving sound around the eight speakers of the performance space. The tape was recorded at the Experimental Studio in Freiburg during two days of intensive co-research with

---

[64] The other three works are *Caminantes ... Ayacucho* (1987), *No hay caminos, hay que caminar ... Andrej Tarkowskij* (1987) and *'Hay que caminar' sognando* (1989).

Kremer in February 1988. In the same way as he had done with Henius over two decades earlier, and following his by now well-established working process, Nono recorded a comprehensive range of Kremer's playing, revealing the full gamut of possible sonorities, attacks and gestures, before final processing and manipulation in the studio. The final tape part was spread across eight channels, focusing on four principal sonic domains: dense materials, electronically and spatially transformed; pure violin sonorities; studio and other ambient sounds and very high violin sounds. The importance of the composer–performer relationship is acknowledged in the title of course; not only are there 'travellers' to accompany Kremer – including the sound technician, who in no way should be considered merely as providing an accompaniment – but there is also a composite portrait of Kremer the musical traveller himself, in search of the sound world that comprises *La lontananza*. Nono too has been a part of this journey of sonic exploration, as with every such experience of co-research with a performer, while temporal (and spatial) travel is implied by the 'madrigal' of the title, evoking the Venetian tradition previously alluded to in *Contrappunto dialettico*. In a sense, the composer, performer and technician are all pilgrims, seeking a spatiotemporal, mobile sound world through joint endeavour, reflecting backwards and forwards through time.

In a series of events worthy of any of Piscator's last-minute production experiences in the 1920s, Nono did not complete the violin part until the day of the world premiere, leaving Kremer only hours to learn the complex part. Although the live part is relatively sparse, it is a technically demanding score, with an equally challenging interface between the violin and tape parts, where each must react to the other while also operating with considerable autonomy, rather in the manner of operation of *A floresta*. The tape neither accompanies nor directs the violin's actions: both are independent, but linked, contributors to the creation of the work. As with *Krapp's Last Tape*, through its staging and performance, the creation of the work happened anew in each live iteration, with Beckett making many adjustments to the work for several years after its world premiere.[65] Although Nono had originally wanted to withdraw the tape part – instead presenting a solo violin world premiere – eventually, the performance went ahead with tape included. Unsatisfied with the result, Nono withdrew the violin part and substantially revised it. Of course, the memory of the original is still present in the new part, and also in the memory of the world premiere itself. *La lontananza* is redolent of Derrida's 'fabric', it passes 'through', sharing textual inspiration with other compositions, generating new materials

---

[65] See Harmon (1998), for Beckett's correspondence with Alan Schneider concerning staging evolution in *Krapp's Last Tape*.

from old processes, and reflecting on the past and the future. In what is practically a hauntological manifesto, its dedicatee, Salvatore Sciarrino, perhaps sums this up best, describing *La lontananza* as 'the past reflected in the present (nostalgica) brings about a creative utopia (utopica); the desire for what is known becomes a vehicle for what will be possible (futura) through the medium of distance (lontananza)' (quoted in Van Eck, 2013, p.3). By combining sound spatialisation and the utilisation of recorded memory, Nono is creating a fundamentally hauntological landscape that shimmers with the traces of traces of traces, simultaneously collapsing and expanding narrative notions of space and time. *La lontananza* embodies Derrida's conceptions of techno-tele-iconicity, techno-tele-discursivity and the spectral moment perhaps better than any of Nono's other compositions, and that in a creative life that was replete with such 'moments'.

Listening to this complete body of work, one is reminded of contemporary hauntologists and their aesthetic practice; their desire to create a certain 'atmosphere' that is redolent of decay and loss, such as the Caretaker's reuse of vintage records of 1930s dance music in *Selected Memories from the Haunted Ballroom* (1999) and *Everywhere at the End of Time* (2016–19), where hiss, crackle and pops form the foundations of the sound world. The very nature of Nono's tape-based studio practice, by now more than fifty years old for much of this repertoire, imbues his sound world with exactly the same qualities that contemporary hauntology adores. Even after restoration and reissue, due to the nature of the recording medium itself and degradation of the original tapes, today the sound world of these works has changed, giving them a hauntological sonic signature that would not have been apparent when they were new; and this 'signature' is even more obvious in compositions where Nono incorporated found objects, such as the records of political speeches in the first part of *Musica-Manifesto no. 1: Un volto, del mare – Non consumiamo Marx*, where pops and crackles are clearly audible on the recordings.

Afterword

By 1988, 'the past reflected in the present' could apply equally to the medium of tape itself. Despite initially holding its own against the blandishments of the compact disc, whose launch in 1982 had already struck the apparent death knell for the record, tape's days were numbered. The advent of midi in 1983, coupled with already existing digital sampling methods, further limited tape's attractiveness as a working format. By the 1990s, CDs had won the battle for the popular market, while composers (and producers) had increasingly moved over to computerised methods of creation, storage and dissemination; the arrival of virtual formats (MP3s) and work methods (DAWs) would dominate the twenty-first century. And yet... forewarnings of tape's demise appear premature. Fast forward to 2002 and William Basinski creates his *The Disintegration Loops* series (2002–3), where tape is foregrounded as an explicitly hauntological medium. Christian Marclay's *Allover (Genesis, Travis Tritt, and others)*, one of a series of cyanotypes produced in 2008, uses unspooled cassette tape as a tool for creating a labyrinth of patterns across the cyanotype's blue field, in a process of mutual change. As the sonic and visual meld, the work's title refers to the musical content of the cassette tapes used to construct the print. In 2011, the Foo Fighters' latest album *Wasting Light* was recorded onto tape, while by 2014, thanks in part to the film *Guardians of the Galaxy* and the central role of the 'awesome mix' as a driver of plot and character, tape had returned to the mainstream. Like vinyl, the cassette tape's wilderness years are currently on hold, and the medium finds itself culturally centre stage once again. Hauntologically, analogue media embodies lost futures and their sonic signature, despite occupying a contemporary – parallel – existence that indicates the possibility of a new future. In a sense, hauntology comprises interlinked acts of mourning – for the medium, its content, justice denied, and a future yet to come – that 'consists always in attempting to ontologize remains, to make them present' (Derrida, 2006, p.9).

But what of performances of mid-century analogue music, how do contemporary performers navigate this complex domain? As an evolving field, there are no precise answers, but the rise of HIP models for acoustic music and HIP's younger cousin HIPEX (historically informed performance of experimental music), led by Luk Vaes and others, have certainly brought questions of analogue organology and other performance materials to the fore. Of course, as both Cage (*Imaginary Landscape No. 1*) and Nono (*A floresta*) were content to allow some pieces to exist in recorded form only, at least for a period of time, one could argue that recorded documents are sufficient. As a lover of the technologically new, it could also be argued that Cage would have wanted to move with the times anyway. However, for a living tradition to continue, performances are needed. For works that require records, even shellac ones, this is not too difficult, especially with the substantial rise of vinyl consumption during the last two decades. It is very easy now to buy a portable machine with inbuilt speakers to perform any work involving records. Tape is slightly more problematic, although it is quite possible to buy vintage machines and tapes to give a realistic simulacrum of the original sound world, and many musicians over the age of forty will still have tape machines, spool tape and cassettes within reach from the first time around. Obsolescence is not confined to analogue media either. Ricordi's current edition of *La fabbrica illuminata*, dating from 2010, provides the restored tape part in a digital format that, although very helpful for the performer, is stored on a DVD. Even by 2020 this was already a somewhat inconvenient format for contemporary performance: a download would be a much more convenient and user-friendly option, while also echoing the convenience of Nono's original portable tape version (without soloist) for use in workers' cooperatives and other lecture events. The different, and for many, superior sound quality of analogue media is an important factor when considering contemporary performance, but it is also worth remembering that analogue has implications for workflow – more advance preparation is required – and variability, as even when new, each piece of physical media, each tape, vinyl or shellac disc, is unique and thus unrepeatable. When natural decay and damage are considered, literally ontologising remains, the variation is considerable, and a fundamental constituent of hauntology's sonic identity. Ultimately, for performers, listeners and creators, these works need to 'live' on, even if they 'live' through the agency of ghosts.

Uniting figures as seemingly disparate as Cage and Nono, one, a Zen-suffused ambivalent anarcho-capitalist, the other, a committed communist, but with reservations about local and global policy, holding sometimes diametrically opposed views on musical matters ranging from improvisation to time, agency to indeterminacy, and the nature of silence, hauntology enables the ghosts of past and future to sit side by side, although perhaps speaking in different languages across this significant body of analogue work. As always, it seems likely that technology will continue to drive creativity forwards, but one is left to wonder, would either Cage or Nono have embraced the current technological trajectory offered by AI, the ultimate dream of the 'not yet', which allows avatars to extend an artist's creative life, to resurrect the dead without consent, to never have to die 'again'?

References

Banita, G. (2010). 'Shadow of the Colossus: The Spectral Lives of 9/11'. In M. D. P. Blanco & E. Peeren, eds., *Popular Ghosts: The Haunted Spaces of Everyday Culture*. London: Continuum, pp.94–105.

Beckett, S. (1990). 'Krapp's Last Tape'. In S. Beckett, ed., *Samuel Beckett: The Complete Dramatic Works*. London: Faber & Faber, pp.213–24.

Benson, E. F. (2012). 'And the Dead Spake –'. In D. S. Davies, ed., *Night Terrors: The Ghost Stories of E. F. Benson*. Ware: Wordsworth Editions, pp.199–216.

Brunette, P. & Wills, D. (1994). 'The Spatial Arts: An Interview with Jacques Derrida'. In P. Brunette & D. Wills, eds., *Deconstruction and the Visual Arts: Art, Media, Architecture*. Cambridge: Cambridge University Press, pp.9–32.

Cage, J. (1960a). *Cartridge Music*. New York: Edition Peters.

Cage, J. (1960b). *Imaginary Landscape No. 1*. New York: Edition Peters. Composed 1939.

Cage, J. (1961a). 'The Future of Music: Credo'. In *Silence: Lectures and Writings*. Middletown, CT: Wesleyan University Press, pp.3–6.

Cage, J. (1961b). *Imaginary Landscape No. 5*. New York: Edition Peters. Composed 1952.

Cage, J. (1961c). *Water Walk*. New York: Edition Peters. Composed 1959.

Cage, J. (1962). *Credo in Us*. New York: Edition Peters. Composed 1942.

Cage, J. (1993). *Composition in Retrospect*. Cambridge, MA: Exact Change.

Cage, J. (2011). *33⅓*. New York: Edition Peters. Composed 1969.

Cage, J. & Feldman, M. (1993). *Radio Happenings: Conversations*. Cologne: MusikTexte.

Caputo, J. D. (1987). *Radical Hermeneutics: Repetition, Deconstruction, and the Hermeneutic Project*. Bloomington: Indiana University Press.

Cecchetto, D. (2013). *Humanesis: Sound and Technological Posthumanism*. Minneapolis: University of Minnesota Press. https://doi.org/10.5749/minnesota/9780816676446.001.0001.

Cossettini, L. (2010). Introduction to *Luigi Nono: La fabbrica illuminata; Critical Edition*. Translated by A. Herklotz. Milan: Ricordi, pp.xxi–xxxvi.

Coverley, M. (2020). *Hauntology: Ghosts of Futures Past*. Harpenden: Oldcastle Books.

Cuntz, M. (2010). 'The Gentle Irruption of the Hereafter in This Life: Jean Echenoz's *Au piano* and Robin Campillo's *Les revenants*'. In M. D. P. Blanco

& E. Peeren, eds., *Popular Ghosts: The Haunted Spaces of Everyday Culture*. London: Continuum, pp.118–32.

De Benedictis, A. I. & Rizzardi, V., eds. (2018). *Nostalgia for the Future: Luigi Nono's Selected Writings and Interviews*. Oakland: University of California Press.

Derrida, J. (1986). 'Bernard Tschumi: La case vide – La Villette 1985. Point de folie – Maintenant l'architecture'. *AA Files*, no. 12 (Summer), pp.65–75.

Derrida, J. (1996). *Archive Fever: A Freudian Impression*. Translated by E. Prenowitz. Chicago, IL: University of Chicago Press.

Derrida, J. (2001). *The Work of Mourning*. Edited by P.-A. Brault & M. Naas. Chicago, IL: University of Chicago Press.

Derrida, J. (2004). 'Plato's Pharmacy'. In *Dissemination*. Translated by B. Johnson. London: Continuum, pp.67–186.

Derrida, J. (2005). *Paper Machine*. Translated by R. Bowlby. Stanford, CA: Stanford University Press.

Derrida, J. (2006). *Specters of Marx: The State of the Debt, the Work of Mourning and the New International*. Translated by P. Kamuf. New York: Routledge.

Derrida, J. (2014). *Cinders*. Translated by N. Lukacher. Introduction by C. Wolfe. Minneapolis: University of Minnesota Press.

Dinwiddie, J. (2011). 'MEWANTEMOOSEICDAY: John Cage in Davis, 1969'. In L. Austin & D. Kahn, eds., *Source: Music of the Avant-Garde, 1966–1973*. Berkeley: University of California Press, pp.234–38.

Fetterman, W. (2010). *John Cage's Theatre Pieces: Notations and Performances*. New York: Routledge. https://doi.org/10.4324/9780203059449.

Fisher, M. (2014). *Ghosts of My Life: Writings on Depression, Hauntology and Lost Futures*. Winchester: Zero Books.

Fisher, M. (2018). *k-punk: The Collected and Unpublished Writings of Mark Fisher (2004–2016)*. Edited by D. Ambrose. London: Repeater Books.

Fukuyama, F. (1992). *The End of History and the Last Man*. London: Penguin.

Garavaglia, R. & Nono, L. (2018). 'Excursus III: Interview with Renato Garavaglia (ca. 1979–80)'. In De Benedictis & Rizzardi, pp.247–62.

Gordon, K. & Marclay, C. (2005). 'Interview: Kim Gordon in Conversation with Christian Marclay'. In J. González, K. Gordon & M. Higgs, eds., *Christian Marclay*. London: Phaidon, pp.6–21.

Grubbs, D. (2014). *Records Ruin the Landscape: John Cage, the Sixties, and Sound Recording*. Durham, NC: Duke University Press. https://doi.org/10.1215/9780822377108.

Hägglund, M. (2008). *Radical Atheism: Derrida and the Time of Life*. Stanford, CA: Stanford University Press.

Harmon, M., ed. (1998). *No Author Better Served: The Correspondence of Samuel Beckett and Alan Schneider*. Cambridge, MA: Harvard University Press.

Heaton, R. (2009). 'Reminder: A Recording Is Not a Performance'. In N. Cook, E. Clarke, D. Leech-Wilkinson & J. Rink, eds., *The Cambridge Companion to Recorded Music*. Cambridge: Cambridge University Press, pp.217–20. https://doi.org/10.1017/CCOL9780521865821.026.

Henius, C. (1991). 'Arbeitsfahrungen mit Luigi Nono als Interpret und Veranstalter'. In O. Kolleritsch, ed., *Die Musik Luigi Nonos*. Vienna: Universal Edition, pp.75–90.

Holmes, T. (2020). *Electronic and Experimental Music: Technology, Music, and Culture*. 6th ed. New York: Routledge. https://doi.org/10.4324/9780429425585.

Iddon, M., ed. (2013). *John Cage and David Tudor: Correspondence on Interpretation and Performance*. Cambridge: Cambridge University Press.

Iddon, M., ed. (2020). *John Cage and Peter Yates: Correspondence on Music Criticism and Aesthetics*. Cambridge: Cambridge University Press. https://doi.org/10.1017/9781108628815.

Impett, J. (2019). *Routledge Handbook to Luigi Nono and Musical Thought*. Abingdon: Routledge.

Innes, C. D. (1972). *Erwin Piscator's Political Theatre: The Development of Modern German Drama*. London: Cambridge University Press.

Kirby, M. & Schechner, R. (1965). 'An Interview with John Cage'. *Tulane Drama Review*, 10(2), 50–72. https://doi.org/10.2307/1125231.

Kostelanetz, R., ed. (1988). *Conversing with Cage*. New York: Limelight Editions.

Kuhn, L., ed. (2016). *The Selected Letters of John Cage*. Middletown, CT: Wesleyan University Press.

Kuhn, L. (2019). 'Foreword: Something of the Beginning'. In L. Kuhn, ed., *Love, Icebox: Letters from John Cage to Merce Cunningham*. New York: John Cage Trust, pp.7–16.

Leach, R. (2006). *Theatre Workshop: Joan Littlewood and the Making of Modern British Theatre*. Exeter: University of Exeter Press.

Marclay, C. (2014). *On&By Christian Marclay*. Edited by J.-P. Criqui. London: Whitechapel Gallery.

Marx, K. & Engels, F. (1985). *The Communist Manifesto*. London: Penguin.

Nanni, M. (2006). 'Ricorda cosa ti hanno fatto in Auschwitz'. Translated by A. Herklotz. Liner note for *Luigi Nono: Complete Works for Solo Tape*. Stradivarius / Ricordi Oggi, STR 57001, 2 compact discs, pp.50–53.

Nielinger-Vakil, C. (2015). *Luigi Nono: A Composer in Context*. Cambridge: Cambridge University Press. https://doi.org/10.1017/CBO9780511842672.

Nono, L. (2010). *La fabbrica illuminata: Critical Edition*. Commentary by L. Cossettini. Milan: Ricordi.

Nono, L. (2018a). '*Die Ermittlung*: A Musical and Theatrical Experience with Weiss and Piscator [Music and Theater] (1966)'. In De Benedictis & Rizzardi, 2018, pp.229–34.

Nono, L. (2018b). 'For Marino Zuccheri (1986)'. In De Benedictis & Rizzardi, 2018, pp.349–58.

Nono, L. (2018c). 'Replies to Seven Questions by Martine Cadieu (1966)'. In De Benedictis & Rizzardi, 2018, pp.277–86.

Piscator, E. (1980). *The Political Theatre*. Translated by H. Rorrison. London: Methuen.

Prati, W., Masotti, R. & Nono, L. (2018). 'Excursus IV. Technology to Discover a Universe of Sounds: Interview with Walter Prati and Roberto Masotti (1983)'. In De Benedictis & Rizzardi, 2018, pp.311–18.

Pritchett, J. (1996). *The Music of John Cage*. Cambridge: Cambridge University Press.

Restagno, E. (2018). 'Excursus I. An Autobiography of the Author Recounted by Enzo Restagno (1987)'. In De Benedictis & Rizzardi, 2018, pp.27–122.

Retallack, J., ed. (1996). *Musicage: Cage Muses on Words, Art, Music*. Hanover, NH: Wesleyan University Press.

Reynolds, S. (2011). *Retromania: Pop Culture's Addiction to Its Own Past*. London: Faber & Faber.

Rizzardi, V. (2006). 'Contrappunto dialettico alla mente'. Translated by A. Herklotz. Liner note for *Luigi Nono: Complete Works for Solo Tape*. Stradivarius / Ricordi Oggi, STR 57001, 2 compact discs, pp.54–62.

Sherburne, P. & Marclay, C. (2014). 'In Conversation with Philip Sherburne, 2005'. In J.-P. Criqui, ed., *On&By Christian Marclay*. London: Whitechapel Gallery, pp.48–53.

Van Eck, H. (2013). 'About the Work'. Liner note for *Luigi Nono: La lontananza nostalgica utopica futura; Hans Van Eck: Nuctemeron*. Sub Rosa, SR309, 1 compact disc & 1 SACD, pp.1–5.

Van Elferen, I. (2010). 'Haunted by a Melody: Ghosts, Transgression, and Music in *Twin Peaks*'. In M. D. P. Blanco & E. Peeren, eds., *Popular Ghosts: The Haunted Spaces of Everyday Culture*. London: Continuum, pp.282–95.

Weiss, P. (1966). *The Investigation: Oratorio in 11 Cantos*. Trans Alexander Gross. London: Marion Boyars.

Wolfe, C. (2014). Introduction to J. Derrida, *Cinders*. Minneapolis: University of Minnesota Press, pp.vii–xxx.

Wortham, S. M. (2010). *The Derrida Dictionary*. London: Continuum.

Cambridge Elements ≡

Music Since 1945

Mervyn Cooke
University of Nottingham

Mervyn Cooke brings to the role of series editor an unusually broad range of expertise, having published widely in the fields of twentieth-century opera, concert and theatre music, jazz, and film music. He has edited and co-edited *Cambridge Companions to Britten, Jazz, Twentieth-Century Opera*, and *Film Music*. His other books include *Britten: War Requiem, Britten and the Far East, A History of Film Music, The Hollywood Film Music Reader, Pat Metheny: The ECM Years*, and two illustrated histories of jazz. He is currently co-editing (with Christopher R. Wilson) *The Oxford Handbook of Shakespeare and Music*.

About the Series

Elements in Music Since 1945 is a highly stimulating collection of authoritative online essays that reflects the latest research into a wide range of musical topics of international significance since the Second World War. Individual Elements are organised into constantly evolving clusters devoted to such topics as art music, jazz, music and image, stage and screen genres, music and media, music and place, immersive music, music and movement, music and politics, music and conflict, and music and society. The latest research questions in theory, criticism, musicology, composition and performance are also given cutting-edge and thought-provoking coverage. The digital-first format allows authors to respond rapidly to new research trends, with contributions being updated to reflect the latest thinking in their fields, and the essays are enhanced by the provision of an exciting range of online resources.

Cambridge Elements

Music Since 1945

Elements in the Series

A Semiotic Approach to Open Notations: Ambiguity as Opportunity
Tristan McKay

Film Music in Concert: The Pioneering Role of the Boston Pops Orchestra
Emilio Audissino

Theory of Prominence: Temporal Structure of Music Based on Linguistic Stress
Bryan Hayslett

Heiner Goebbels and Curatorial Composing after Cage: From Staging Works to Musicalising Encounters
Ed McKeon

Understanding Stockhausen
Robin Maconie

The Queerness of Video Game Music
Tim Summers

Olivier Messiaen's Turangalîla-symphonie
Andrew Shenton

Chinese Émigré Composers and Divergent Modernisms: Chen Yi and Zhou Long
Mia Chung

Mariachi in the Twenty-First Century
Donald A. Westbrook

Elliott Carter's String Quartet No. 1: Myths, Narratives, and Cold War Cultural Diplomacy
Laura Emmery

Rhythm and Heritage in Modern Flamenco Guitar
Carlos van Tongeren

Cage, Nono and 1960s Hauntology: Sonic Ghosts
Clare Lesser

A full series listing is available at: www.cambridge.org/EM45

For EU product safety concerns, contact us at Calle de José Abascal, 56–1°, 28003 Madrid, Spain or eugpsr@cambridge.org.